ANIMAL IDIOMS

Jeff Garrison
Masahiko Goshi

KODANSHA INTERNATIONAL
Tokyo • New York • London

Distributed in the United States by Kodansha America, Inc., 114 Fifth Avenue, New York, N.Y. 10011, and in the United Kingdom and continental Europe by Kodansha Europe Ltd., 95 Aldwych, London WC2B 4JF. Published by Kodansha International Ltd., 17-14 Otowa 1-chome, Bunkyo-ku, Tokyo 112, and Kodansha America, Inc.

First edition, 1996
96 97 98 99 10 9 8 7 6 5 4 3 2 1
ISBN 4-7700-1668-9

CONTENTS

PREFACE

Stop for a moment to think of the last time you heard someone say that he "stirred up a hornet's nest" by asking why the boss's son got the nod before he did, or the last time you heard a friend gripe about "the tail wagging the dog" when she heard politicians pontificate about what was best for the nation. You may even have egged on a rowdy drinking buddy by telling him that the fast-approaching 220-pound bouncer everyone called "Hulk" was really just a big ol' "pussycat."

Most English speakers have heard these and hundreds of other "beastly" expressions in daily conversation, and with this book, students of Japanese, many of whom are already convinced that Japan is a zoo, now have linguistic proof that the wild kingdom is alive and well in the language if not the land of their study. Japanese has accumulated a linguistic menagerie over the ages that is as wide-ranging as the sea, land, and sky that nurtures the national consciousness and has given generations of Japanese wags food for thought as well as the palate. Surprisingly, some idioms are precisely the same as their English equivalent: *karasu no ashiato* for those pesky "crows feet" around the corners of your aging eyes, *mizu o hanareta sakana* to describe someone who is out of his element or "like a fish out of water." Other linguistic "animalisms" seem to have arisen from observation of similar traits in different beasts: *kamo* (duck) for every gambler's dream, the "pigeon"; or *yabuhebi*, shortened from *yabu o tsutsuite hebi o dasu*, or literally, "poke around in the brush and drive out a snake," or "stir up a hornet's nest."

Still other expressions arise from unique, fanciful observations of animality. *Ushi no yodare* (cow saliva), for example, is used of something that drags on interminably, while *kingyo no fun* (goldfish poop) is a graphic depiction of someone you want badly to shake but who just keeps hanging on. Finally there are the seeming conundrums: *bōfura ga waku* (mosquito larva swarm), for instance, stumped one of the authors the first time he heard it. Of course, he was already three sheets to the wind after an evening of elbow bending when his buddy smilingly motioned with a beer bottle to top off his glass and said, *"Nomanai to bōfura ga waku zo,"* alluding to mosquitos hatching on a stagnant pool, as an encouragement to "drink up" before the beer in his glass went flat.

Whatever the source of inspiration, the result is often an addition to the language that can focus attention, invite mirth, and occasionally encourage reflection on the linguistic importance of the wild kingdom to our daily lives. All this despite the distressing dearth of wildlife, especially mammalian, in present-day Japan, for even a cursory survey of the language shows that that the nation has not always been so bereft of furry, flying or scaly creatures. Evidence that past generations of Japanese lived in closer proximity to the natural world abounds in the myriad of colorful idioms and maxims that include mammals, amphibians, reptiles, birds, fishes and insects, many of which idioms have been handed down to the present from the distant past. Indeed, after a preliminary survey, the authors concluded that fauna had wiggled and wormed their way deeply into the national consciousness in so many colorful and ingenious ways that we set about convincing our editors at Kodansha International of the *need* for a book enumerating and explaining (when possible) how it was that so many critters had taken up residence in the language.

We have selected a good many, but by no means all, the outstanding representatives of both the wild and not-so-wild kingdoms for inclusion. They are first organized loosely under class and then in the traditional Japanese あいうえお fashion. Under "Mammals," for example, *kujira* (whale) comes before *kuma* (bear). When an animal, bird, fish, or insect appears in more than one idiom it is included under the one which comes first. *Uma o ushi ni kaeru* would thus appear under *uma* (horse) rather than *ushi* (cow).

まえがき

1979年のECの秘密文書に、日本の住宅事情を「兎小屋 (rabbit hutch) に住む日本人」という表現があり、物議をかもした。ヨーロッパの人もよく言ったものだが、でもこれではまだあまい、わが日本語にはもっとピッタリくる表現がある。何たって、「猫の額」(A piece of ground so small you can't even swing a cat) 程の土地が何億円、「鰻の寝床」(a long, narrow place) や「豚小屋」(a pigpen, pigsty) のような部屋に住んでいる日本人も少なくない。毎日すし詰めの通勤電車に乗って、「馬車馬のように働く」(work like dog) 人や、「独楽鼠のように働く」(work one's tail off) われわれの姿を、外国の人々にいわれる前にうまいこと英語で表現できたら国際理解も結構進むのではないか。

言葉を理解することは同時にその文化を知ることというが、この東西の文化は似たような表現もすれば、全く違った発想を発見することもある。「犬が西向きゃ尾は東」(この意味が分からない日本人は是非この本を買うことをおすすめします)、英語では "熊" が登場する。"Does a bear shit in the woods?"(熊は森で糞たれる？)――英語は下品だと思いの方、日本語も負けてはいません。結婚式のスピーチで困るのが「牛の小便」みたいなやつ。英語では "drone on (forever)" というが、ところでこの "drone" という言葉、ここでは「長々と話す」という意味ですが、「蜂がブンブンと音を立てる」という意味もある。同じ生き物を使ったものでも、その使い方に発想の違いを見い出すことができる。

その一方でこの何万キロも離れた二つの文化で同じ様な表現を発見すると、「鳥肌」の立つ思いをするのは著者だけか

も知れないが、英語では "goose pimples"（ガチョウの肌）と表現する。そう言えば、彼の有名なアーチスト、クインシー・ジョーンズも "Torihada, tori hada mono" とこの言葉が気に入ったように使っているのをラジオで聴いたことがある。ところで、気に入った表現はなるべく早く実際に使ってみるのが言葉を覚えるコツである。六本木あたりのカラオケで "Your husky voice gives me goose bumps" なんて試してみたら結構おもしろいかも…。

　本書では動物を使った表現をそれぞれ哺乳類、爬虫類と両生類、昆虫、魚介類、鳥類に分類しアイウエオ順に収録した。日本語と英語の例文でその使い方を分かりやすく紹介しています。

SYMBOLS ────────────────────────────

The following symbols are used in this book.

☞   marks the introduction to a particular animal

●   marks a main entry for an idiom, with Japanese
    script, romanization, literal meaning, and (on the
    following line) English equivalents

○   marks sample sentences or short dialogues illus-
    trating an idiom, with Japanese script, romaniza-
    tion, and English translation

※   marks a comment on the preceding idiom

❧   marks a synonym that appears elsewhere in the
    book

❧   marks an antonym that appears elsewhere in the
    book

I

哺乳類
MAMMALS

Judging from the preponderance of idioms with mammals in them, you might expect the islands to be a veritable mammalian menagerie, one awash in the bloodcurdling crys of attacking predators and dying prey, or at least some decent ungulate roadkill, legs stiff and pointing skyward. Think again. While there are said to be over a hundred land-dwelling mammals in Japan, you could go through your whole life and never see anything more exotic than a cat or a cow, and you would have to look hard for the latter.

A closer look at the idioms, however, reveals that domestic animals dominate the bestial lexicon, and for good reason, for it is the proximity of dogs and cats, as well as cows and horses, to humans that makes for familiarity and allows the behavioral observations so crucial to the formation of the pithy and picturesque.

いたち（鼬） *itachi* weasel

☞ Not exactly man's best friend in Japan, the weasel comes off little better in Japanese than in English. Like the fox, it is believed to be the harbinger of bad luck when encountered and was formerly thought to breathe fire. As can be inferred from the examples below, it is believed to be mischievous and cunning. Weasels are counted *ippiki* 一匹.

● いたちごっこ *itachi-gokko* "play weasel"
the cat and mouse game; (go) round and round

○ 東京の路上駐車の問題は、警察とドライバーのいたちごっこに終わっている。

Tōkyō no rojō-chūsha no mondai wa, keisatsu to doraibā no itachi-gokko ni owatte iru.

There's no end in sight to the endless game of cat and mouse played out on the streets of Tokyo between police and drivers who park illegally.

○ ハッカーとの長年のいたちごっこを終結に向かわせる研究にメーカーは注目している。

Hakkā to no naganen no itachi-gokko o shūketsu ni mukawaseru kenkyū ni mēkā wa chūmoku shite iru.

Manufacturers are pinning their hopes on research that promises to bring an end to years of going round and round with hackers.

🐾 Derived from a very primitive form of one-upsmanship, idiomatic usage of *itachi-gokko* has its origins in a game by the same name played by children in the late Edo period in which two children face each other and repeat the phrase *itachi-gokko, nezumi-gokko* (play weasel, play rat) while pinching the back of the other's extended hands and placing their own on top to have it pinched in return until the stack rises out of reach, or until they lose interest or can no longer bear the pain (which usually comes first). The game possibly developed from the observation of the struggle for survival between the weasel and its prey the rat. The term -*gokko* is a suffix meaning play or game, as in *oisha-san-gokko* お医者さんごっこ, or play doctor.

● いたちの最後っぺ　*itachi no saigoppe*　"a weasel's last fart"
a parting shot, a last gasp retort; a last ditch effort

○ いたちの最後っぺよろしく、彼は会社の秘密を暴露して、辞めて行った。

Itachi no saigoppe yoroshiku, kare wa kaisha no himitsu o bakuro shite, yamete itta.

His parting shot upon quitting was to expose corporate secrets.

○ 泥棒は、いたちの最後っぺよろしく、盗んだ金の一部をバラまいて捜査員の追尾を振り切ろうとした。

Dorobō wa, itachi no saigoppe yoroshiku, nusunda kane no ichibu o baramaite sōsa-in no tsuibi o furikirō to shita.

The thief scattered some of the money he had stolen in a last ditch effort to throw the police off his trail.

🐾 From the weasel's documented ability to emit a foul odor from its anal glands when all other means of escape have failed. The expression is frequently used with *yoroshiku*, which means "just like."

犬 *inu* dog

☞ Dogs have been hanging around long enough to warrant mention in the *Kojiki,* Japan's oldest extant historical work. And although they figure in numerous expressions, the images elicited are generally the result of the dog's inferior qualities.

Incidentally, Japanese dog lovers—well, actually the pet food industry—made November 1, 1987 (that's day *wan* of the *wan-wan* month, for the uninitiated), and every November 1 thereafter, official Dog Day, choosing the day because the dog's bark is written *wan-wan* ワンワン, and *wan* is about as close to "one" as they could get in the native syllabary. So why didn't they make it January first, eh? Hey, who knows. Wonder why native speakers of English haven't made those sultry days of summer we know as "dog days" some kind of monument to dogdom, too? Could be that Western petfood makers are happy just to gouge pet owners without making fools of them to boot.

An interesting insight into how man's best friend was thought of in earlier days can be gained from a look at the word for a useless or shameless samurai, *inuzamurai* 犬侍, or a dog samurai. The word possibly derives from the fact that dogs, unlike domesticated animals such as cows or horses, are relatively unproductive and, according to one source, display a particularly beastly lack of decorum by copulating in public.

In addition to the more common *koinu* 小犬 puppies are also called *inukoro* 犬ころ. Large or small, the canine bark is *wan-wan* ワンワン in Japanese. They are counted *ippiki* 一匹 or *ittō* 一頭.

Written 戌, the dog is eleventh among the twelve signs of the Chinese zodiac.

● 犬 *inu* "dog"
a (police) spy, mole, plant, an informant, a shamus; asslicker, a brown-noser, cat's paw, flunky, lackey, sycophant, stooge, stool pigeon, toady, yes-man; a slave (to the passions)

○ おまえ一生政府の犬でいるつもりか。
Omae isshō seifu no inu de iru tsumori ka.
Are you gonna spend your whole life informing for the government?

○ あいつは社長の犬だから、気をつけて話せよ。
Aitsu wa shachō no inu da kara, ki o tsukete hanase yo.
Watch out when you talk to that guy. He's the boss's lackey.

○ おまえいつからあんな奴の犬に成り下がったんだ。
Omae itsu kara anna yatsu no inu ni narisagatta n' da.

Since when have you fallen so low that you're ratting on your friends for him?

○ あいつはどうも犬のような気がする。
Aitsu wa dōmo inu no yō na ki ga suru.
I get the feeling the guy's a plant.

○ おまえが（警察の）犬だということがばれたらコンクリート詰めだぞ。
Omae ga (keisatsu no) inu da to iu koto ga baretara konkurīto-zume da zo.
You'll end up dressed in concrete if word ever gets out that you're working for the pigs.

❦ Often written in katakana, this use of *inu* is possibly from the dog's quality of compliance to its owner's wishes.

● 犬かき　*inukaki*　"dog scratching"
dog paddle

○ 俺犬かきしかできないんだ。
Ore inukaki shika dekinai n' da.
The only thing I can do is dog-paddle.

○ 競泳パンツで犬かきしてたのを友人たちに見られて稔は二度と海水浴に行くことはなかった。
Kyōei-pantsu de inukaki shite 'ta no o yūjin-tachi ni mirarete Minoru wa nido to kaisui-yoku ni iku koto wa nakatta.
Minoru never went to the beach again after his friends caught him dog-paddling in a pair of really cool Speedos.

❦ Also, but less commonly, *inu-oyogi* 犬泳.

● 犬が西向きゃ尾は東　*inu ga nishi mukya o wa higashi*　"a dog's tail points east when the dog points west"
obviously; needless to say; Does a cat have an ass? Is Stevie Wonder blind?

○ 犬が西向きゃ尾は東、卒業なんか無理だよ。学校に行ってないんだから。
Inu ga nishi mukya o wa higashi, sotsugyō nanka muri da yo. Gakkō ni itte 'nai n' da kara.
It's no surprise that you're not going to graduate. You never go to class.

○ 彼女は「犬が西向きゃ尾は東」式のことしか会議で発言しない。
Kanojo wa "Inu ga nishi mukya o wa higashi" shiki no koto shika kaigi de hatsugen shinai.
The only remarks she made at the meeting were of the most obvious sort, like the sun rises in the east.

○ そういうの、犬が西向きゃ尾は東っていうんだよ。
Sō iu no, inu ga nishi mukya o wa higashi tte iu n' da yo.
Does a bear shit in the woods?

✌ As can be seen in the last example, like similar English retorts, this expression is also used in response to a comment the speaker feels is patently true or false. Unlike its English equivalents, this and similar Japanese expressions are seldom used as rhetorical responses to a question by another person.

● 犬死に　*inuji ni*　"a dog's death"
die a dog's death, die in vain

○ 彼は結局犬死にした。
Kare wa kekkyoku inuji ni shita.
He died like a dog in the end.

○ 彼は過労死したにもかかわらず、賠償金はわずかで、会社のために犬死にしたことになった。
Kare wa karō-shi shita ni mo kakawarazu, baishō-kin wa wazuka de, kaisha no tame ni inuji ni shita koto ni natta.
Despite the fact that overwork killed him, the company paid such a piddling sum in damages that his death was truly in vain.

✌ Although appearing most commonly in verb form, *inuji ni suru,* it can also be used to express futility or effort that goes unrewarded. In such cases, it is followed by *dōzen* 同然, as in the following example:

それじゃあ、犬死に同然だ。
Sore jā, inuji ni dōzen da.
That amounts to throwing away your life for nothing.

● 犬畜生　*inu-chikushō*　"a dog from hell"
a beast, a cur

○ あいつは犬畜生にも劣る。
Aitsu wa inu-chikushō ni mo otoru.
He's lower than pond scum.

○ 犬畜生だってそんなことはしないよ。
Inu-chikushō datte sonna koto wa shinai yo.
Even a lowly cur wouldn't do something like that.

𝄆 Obviously derogatory, the word can be used in response to a person's speech or behavior.

● 犬も歩けば棒に当たる   *inu mo arukeba bō ni ataru* "if a dogs walks around enough, it is likely to get hit with a stick"
1. (of bad fortune) trouble lurks, be out of luck

○ 「犬も歩けば棒に当たる」で散歩してたら頭に鳥の糞が落ちてきた。
"Inu mo arukeba bō ni ataru" de sanpo shite 'tara atama ni tori no fun ga ochite kita.
Some bird shit on my head when I went out for a walk. Guess it just wasn't my day.

○ 昨日の夜はまさに「犬も歩けば棒に当たる」で、渋谷で得体の知れない奴らに金をせびられた。
Kinō no yoru wa masa ni "Inu mo arukeba bō ni ataru" de, Shibuya de etai no shirenai yatsura ni kane o sebirareta.
You really just never know what's gonna happen. There I was out walking around Shibuya, minding my own business last night, when a bunch of guys I didn't know from Adam came up and started hassling me for money.

---

2. (of good fortune) every dog has his day, be in luck, be *one's* lucky day

---

○ 昨日は犬も歩けば棒に当たるで、パチンコで結構稼いだよ。
Kinō wa inu mo arukeba bō ni ataru de, pachinko de kekkō kaseida yo.
I made out like a bandit yesterday playing pachinko. Hey, it's like they say, every dog has his day.

○ 犬も歩けば棒に当たるだよ、いいバイトが見つかった。
Inu mo arukeba bō ni ataru da yo, ii baito ga mitsukatta.
I lucked into this great part-time job.

𝄆 Dogs and their human friends are likely to meet with something unexpected if they are active in anyway at all. It is obviously safer for one and all to stay home in bed. Of the definitions above, the second and more recent meaning derives from a mistaken use of the phrase, and now appears to be more common than the original.

● 犬も食わない　*inu mo kuwanai*　"even a dog will turn up its nose"

avoid *something* like the plague; won't touch *something* with a ten-foot pole

○ 夫婦喧嘩は犬も食わない。
Fūfu-genka wa inu mo kuwanai.
No one in his right mind wants to get mixed up in someone else's marital spat.

○ そんなくだらない話犬も食わないよ。
Sonna kudaranai hanashi inu mo kuwanai yo.
I can't imagine anyone showing any interest in something that stupid.

𝄞 Derives from the observation that dogs are notoriously omnivorous, and if a dog won't touch something, it has to be pretty bad. It appears only in the negative, and predominately in reference to domestic quarrels.

● 飼い犬に手を噛まれる　*kaiinu ni te o kamareru*　"be bitten by one's pet dog"

be double-crossed (stabbed in the back) by someone trusted; warm a snake in one's bosom

○ 山川の独立は社長にとってまさに飼い犬に手を噛まれた出来事だった。
Yamakawa no dokuritsu wa shachō ni totte masa ni kaiinu ni te o kamareta dekigoto datta.
Yamakawa going independent was seen as an act of betrayal by the boss.

○ マネージャーに金を横領されたタレントは飼い犬に手を噛まれたと有名になった。
Manējā ni kane o ōryō sareta tarento wa kaiinu ni te o kamareta to yūmei ni natta.
Some celebrity got a lot of press for being double-crossed by her manager, who was embezzling money from her.

𝄞 Used when the one doing the betraying is a trusted subordinate or someone otherwise indebted to the person betrayed. Similar to the English expression "bite the hand that feeds *one*," but the Japanese version is always used from the point of view of the person having their hand bitten.

● 犬猿（犬と猿）の仲　*ken-en (inu to saru) no naka* "dog-and-monkey relationship"
be at each other all the time, get along like a cat and a dog; be bad blood between

---

○ 伊藤さんと鈴木さんは犬猿の仲だ。
Itō-san to Suzuki-san wa ken-en no naka da.
There's bad blood between Ito and Suzuki.

○ 環境保護団体と大企業は往々にして犬と猿である。
Kankyōhogo-dantai to dai-kigyō wa ōō ni shite inu to saru de aru.
Environmental groups and big business are always going round and round like cats and dogs.

📖 The two variations of this idiom appear to enjoy similar frequency of use, though some sources claim the former may be slightly more common. Idiomatic usage is thought to have originated from the Japanese fairy tale *Momotarō* 「桃太郎」 in which two retainers, a dog and a monkey, began to fight over the reward after the ogre had been banished to an outlying island.

● 負け犬　*makeinu* "defeated dog"
a loser, failure, down-and-outer, an also-ran; a nobody

○ おまえのような負け犬はこのチームにはいらない。
Omae no yō na makeinu wa kono chīmu ni wa iranai.
We don't need losers like you on the team.

○ 負け犬になったらおしまいだよ。君のように上を狙っている奴がうようよしているんだから。
Makeinu ni nattara oshimai da yo. Kimi no yō ni ue o neratte iru yatsu ga uyouyo shite iru n' da kara.
If you tuck your tail between your legs and give up now, it's curtains for you. There are all kinds of people out there just like you who are trying to get on top.

📖 This is not used of a person or team considered unlikely to compete successfully in a future event, someone referred to in English as an underdog. *Makeinu* is used of one who has already, often habitually, lost and has the air of failure about him. It comes from the image of a dog in full retreat, tail tucked between its legs, after losing a fight.

● 負け犬の遠吠え　*makeinu no tōboe* the howling of a defeated dog

a parting shot; an empty threat; (leave a person with) a few menacing words

○ 加藤のせりふは負け犬の遠吠え以外の何ものでもなかった。

Katō no serifu wa makeinu no tōboe igai no nanimono de mo nakatta.

All that stuff Kato was saying was nothing but a bunch of sour grapes.

○ 配置転換を批判する彼の言葉は負け犬の遠吠えに聞こえなくもない。

Haichi-tenkan o hihan suru kare no kotoba wa makeinu no tōboe ni kikoenaku mo nai.

His complaints about being transferred sound like so much whining.

🐾 Of what people who have been defeated or humiliated say when they are unable to back up their words with action. From the observation that a dog defeated by another retreats, tail between its legs, to howl in the distance.

いのしし（猪）　*inoshishi*　wild boar

☞ Hunted since ancient times in Japan, this stout omnivore is known for the havoc it wreaks on crops as well as its mad rushes and observed inability to change direction quickly. The compound *inoshishi-musha* 猪武者 was formerly used to describe a reckless samurai and through the years has been applied to anyone who rushes headlong into things without considering the consequences.

The meat, variously called *yamakujira* (mountain whale—from earlier days when consumption of wild meat was taboo but whale meat accepted) and *botan* (peony), is rarely seen in Japan today and is therefore prized.

Wild boars are counted *ittō* 一頭 or *ippiki* 一匹. Written 亥, the boar is twelfth among the twelve signs of the Chinese zodiac.

● 猪突猛進　*chototsu-mōshin*　"the boar's wild rush"

reckless, foolhardy, madcap; straight ahead (and damn the torpedos)

○ 猪突猛進の彼にこの仕事を任せない方がいい。

Chototsu-mōshin no kare ni kono shigoto o makasenai hō ga ii.

He's so foolhardy that we'd better not put him in charge of this project.

○ 彼女の性格は一言で言うと猪突猛進型です。

Kanojo no seikaku wa hitokoto de iu to chototsu-mōshin-gata desu.
You could characterize her personality in a word, "reckless."

⚘ From the way a wild boar runs straight ahead full-blast, looking neither right nor left, and its inability to change directions quickly. Not the kind of thing you'd want to have somebody say about you.

うさぎ（兎）　*usagi*　rabbit, hare

☞ Rabbitry has been in the myth, folklore, and language of Japan since at least the early 700s, when mentioned in the *Kojiki*. Considered a trickster, the rabbit also figures as the Japanese equivalent of the English "Man in the Moon," for some still hold that a rabbit can be seen hard at work pounding *mochi* on the face of a full moon. Only a few species exist in Japan today and, although they are equally prolific, Japanese rabbits have yet to achieve the same notoriety for copulating as they have in English.

Rabbits are counted *ippiki* 一匹 or, of all things, *ichiwa* 一羽, no doubt because of the size or resemblance of their ears to wings and some distant flight of fancy that found common ground with birds, which are normally counted in this way. Written 卯 , the hare is fourth among the twelve signs of the Chinese zodiac.

● うさぎ小屋　*usagigoya*　"a rabbit hut"
a rabbit hutch, warren

○ うさぎ小屋に住みたくて日本人は住んでいるんじゃないよ。
Usagigoya ni sumitakute Nihon-jin wa sunde iru n' ja nai yo.
Japanese don't live in small, cramped "rabbit hutches" because they want to, you know.

○ こんなうさぎ小屋に住むなんて、もうこりごりだ。
Konna usagigoya ni sumu nante, mō korigori da.
I'm sick and tired of living in a warren like this.

⚘ It was in 1979 that information from a confidential EC document containing the English expression was leaked to the press. The observation by an undiplomatic foreign diplomat that Japanese were living in rabbit hutches caused an uproar in Kasumigaseki, particularly within the Construction Ministry. Of course, the stoic Japanese citizenry was being told nothing they hadn't already known firsthand for generations, a fact which caused them to look upon Japanese officialdom's righteous indignation somewhat sardonically.

● うさぎ跳び　*usagitobi*　"a rabbit hop"
hop with one's hands clasped behind one's back

○ よし、1年生はうさぎ跳び100回だ。
Yoshi, ichinen-sei wa usagitobi hyakkai da.
All right all you freshmen, I want to see a hundred rabbit hops right now.

○ あいつうさぎ跳び200回やっても涼しい顔してる。
Aitsu usagitobi nihyakkai yatte mo suzushii kao shite 'ru.
He can do 200 rabbit hops and still look as cool as a cucumber.

✌ From the physical resemblance of this activity to a rabbit in motion.

● とにかく（兎に角）　*tonikaku*　"horns on a rabbit"
anyway, anyhow, in any case, at any rate, either way, even so, be that as it may

---

○ とにかく、彼に尋ねてみよう。
Tonikaku, kare ni tazunete miyō.
Anyway, I'll just ask him and see what's up.

○ とにかく、これ食べてごらんよ、美味しいから。
Tonikaku, kore tabete goran yo, oishii kara.
Don't give me that, just try it. It's really good.

○ とにかく、彼女は強情だ。
Tonikaku, kanojo wa gōjō da.
At any rate, she's one hard-headed woman.

✌ The characters for rabbit and horn are said to be merely phonetic equivalents, though it is not a great leap to the notion that even in the unlikely event that rabbits were found to have horns, the speaker would still hold such-and-such to be the case, i.e., anyhow. But this is idle speculation.

うし（牛）　*ushi*　COW

☞ The fact that cattle have been plodding around Japan for the last two thousand years or so goes a long way toward explaining why these bovines figure so largely in the language. Their size, appetite, docility, and reputation for lethargy, as well as their observed ability to trample unsuspecting human fry underfoot all figure in idioms included herein.

These beasts of burden were long free from fear of being butchered because of Buddhist proscriptions, but in modern Japan, beginning in the Meiji period, domestic beef has been piled increasingly higher on the tables of the nation. In one Kansai area, the Matsuzaka breed is even fed beer to fatten it up, while marbling and softening its meat. Matsuzaka beef remains highly prized—and exorbitantly priced in today's competitive market.

The cow's moo is *mōmō* モウモウ, and cows, bulls, and calves are counted *ippiki* 一匹 or *ittō* 一頭. Written 丑, the cow is second among the twelve signs of the Chinese zodiac.

● 牛のよだれ　*ushi no yodare*　"cow drool"
long and slow; slower than molasses in January

○ うちの社長の訓辞はいつも牛のよだれのようだ。
Uchi no shachō no kunji wa itsumo ushi no yodare no yō da.
Our president's little pep talks are always such ho-hummers.

○ 会議はなぜいつも牛のよだれのようなのだろうか。
Kaigi wa naze itsumo ushi no yodare no yō na no darō ka.
Why are meetings always so long and drawn out?

❦ Most commonly of desultory discourse. Almost always followed by *no yō*.

❧ *ushi no shōben* 牛の小便

● 牛の小便　*ushi no shōben*　"cow piss"
unending, long and drawn out

○ あの牛の小便みたいな街頭演説やめてくれないかなあ。
Ano ushi no shōben mitai na gaitō-enzetsu yamete kurenai ka nā.
I sure wish they'd do away with those campaign speeches that just seem to go on and on.

○ あの先生いったん説教を始めると牛の小便でうんざりだ。
Ano sensei ittan sekkyō o hajimeru to ushi no shōben de unzari da.
I'm sick of the way that once that prof starts in on us he drones on forever.

❦ This picturesque idiom is used of interminable things, usually of speeches that just don't seem to end.

❧ *ushi no yodare* 牛のよだれ

● 牛耳る　*gyūjiru*　"grasp a cow's ear"
control, dominate, hold sway over; take charge of, lead, run (the show), shepherd, steer

○ 現在、日本の政界を牛耳る人物がいない。

Genzai, Nihon no seikai o gyūjiru jinbutsu ga inai.

No single person rides herd over the Japanese political world right now.

○ 一部の人間に牛耳られたあの会社には将来は望めないだろう。

Ichibu no ningen ni gyūjirareta ano kaisha ni wa shōrai wa nozomenai darō.

Controlled by a small group of people, a company like that doesn't have much of a future.

🐃 Shortened and made into a verb from the expression *gyūji o toru* 牛耳 を執る, literally "grasp a cow's ear," this is exactly what the fabled feudal rulers of ancient China are said to have done at a meeting where they swore allegiance to one another at the behest of the leading member of the alliance, who then cut off the ear of a sacrificial cow, divided it up among those in attendance, and each of them sucked blood from their share of the dismembered ear. Sort of a different twist to a blood oath, less painful for all except the cow.

● 牛歩（牛の歩み） *gyūho (ushi no ayumi)* "a cow's gait" a very slow walk; last-ditch stalling (slow-down) tactics [in parliament]

○ 野党はその法案に反対の立場から、投票に牛歩戦術で対抗した。

Yatō wa sono hōan ni hantai no tachiba kara, tōhyō ni gyūho-senjutsu de taikō shita.

The opposition party resorted to plodding up to cast its ballots when the bill it opposed came to (up for) a vote.

○ 美術館の行列は牛の歩みだった。

Bijutsu-kan no gyōretsu wa ushi no ayumi datta.

The line at the art museum was moving at a snail's pace.

🐃 This expression is most commonly used to describe one of the more senseless if amusing tactics employed by an outnumbered opposition party in the lower house of Japan's Diet. Facing certain defeat, members of the minority party line up to cast their ballots against a bill and proceed to plod toward the ballot box in the chamber by walking more slowly than the beasts of burden from which the expression takes its inspiration. Hours can pass, seasons come and go, and mountains tumble into the sea before the foregone conclusion, defeat, is official. It's a great argument for live coverage of the Diet, and gives new meaning to voting with your feet.

うま（馬） *uma* horse

☞ Archaeological evidence indicates that the horse may have been introduced to Japan as long ago as the Jōmon period. Formerly considered to be the chosen means of transportation of the gods, horses have long served as draft animals, military mounts, and expensive hors d'oeuvres. More recently, young women have taken to betting on them, instead of burning their bras.

The horse's whinny is *hihīn* ヒヒーン in Japanese. Horses are counted *ippiki* 一匹 or *ittō* 一頭. Written 午, the horse is seventh among the twelve signs of the Chinese zodiac.

● 当て馬　*ateuma*　"an applied horse"
a plant, decoy; (of a political candidate sent out to test the waters or divide the opposition) a stalking horse, a spoiler

---

○ 当て馬を使って相手の出方を見てみよう。
Ateuma o tsukatte aite no dekata o mite miyō.
Let's see if we can draw them out by sending in a decoy.

○ あの人は単に当て馬候補にされただけさ。
Ano hito wa tan ni ateuma kōho ni sareta dake sa.
That candidate's just a stalking horse.

✌ Metaphoric use derives from the original meaning of a stallion used to discover or encourage the readiness of a mare to mate.

● 馬が合う　*uma ga au*　"the horse fits"
get along (get on) well (with each other), be on the same wavelength, click

---

○ 俺、馬が合うんだよあの人とは。
Ore, uma ga au n' da yo ano hito to wa.
I get along great with him.

○ 最初から馬が合ったその二人はトントン拍子で結婚した。
Saisho kara uma ga atta sono futari wa tonton byōshi de kekkon shita.
The two of them hit it off right from the start and sailed straight into marriage.

○ 山川部長と社長はどうも馬が合わないようだ。
Yamakawa buchō to shachō wa dōmo uma ga awanai yō da.
Department head Yamakawa and the CEO just don't seem to be on the same wavelength.

🐾 In the negative form, *uma ga awanai,* this expression is similiar to *mushi ga sukanai* 虫が好かない. Care should be taken, however, in distinguishing the two, for while the former can be used by the speaker about two third-parties who do not get along, use of the latter is limited to the relationship between the speaker and a third party and is not used to describe how others feel toward one another. Insofar as it expresses feelings of incompatibility, *uma ga awanai* shares common ground with *inusaru no naka* 犬猿の仲, another expression included in this book.

● 馬面 *umazura* "a horseface"
a horseface, (literally) a long face

○ 彼は馬面だ。
Kare wa umazura da.
He has a face like a horse. / He's horse-faced.

○ あの役者は馬面だから舞台映えする。
Ano yakusha wa umazura da kara butai-bae suru.
Guy's got one big ol' face; just right for the stage.

🐾 Used exclusively to describe or mock an elongated face, not to describe one as appearing unhappy.

● 馬の骨 *uma no hone* "horse bones"
a mystery man, (rarely and not within the context of marriage) a mystery woman; a person from nowhere, a nobody

○ どこの馬の骨だ、お前と結婚したいと言っているのは。
Doko no uma no hone da, omae to kekkon shitai to itte iru no wa.
So exactly who is this character who says he wants to marry you?

○ どこの馬の骨ともわからない奴に娘をやるぐらいなら一生俺が面倒見てやる。
Doko no uma no hone tomo wakaranai yatsu ni musume o yaru gurai nara isshō ore ga mendō mite yaru.
I'd rather look after my daughter for the rest of my life than see her married off to some Joe Schmo.

○ どこの馬の骨ともわからない奴に会社を乗っ取られてたまるか。
Doko no uma no hone to mo wakaranai yatsu ni kaisha o nottorarete tamaru ka.
I'm not putting up with some guy outa' nowhere coming in and taking over the company!

🐾 Often immediately preceded by *doko no*, this idiom is most commonly wielded by irate fathers about to lose their beloved daughters to suitors

whom they are unwilling to recognize. Pejorative reference to the unknown origin or parentage of the male suitor. It is this sense of "suitor"
that makes the final example possible.

● 馬の耳に念仏 *uma no mimi ni nenbutsu* "(chanting) the
prayer to Amida Buddha in a horse's ear"
(like) preaching to the wind, preaching to deaf ears; (like)
water off a duck's back, whistling in the wind

○ もうけ主義の会社に、資源保護を訴えても、馬の耳に念仏だ。
*Mōke-shugi no kaisha ni, shigen-hogo o uttaete mo, uma no mimi
ni nenbutsu da.*
Appealing for environmental protection measures to corporations
bent on maximizing profits is like preaching to the wind.

○ 暴走族に騒音防止を唱えても、それこそ馬の耳に念仏じゃないか。
*Bosō-zoku ni sōon-bōshi o tonaete mo, sore koso uma no mimi ni
nenbutsu ja nai ka.*
Talking to motorcycle gangs about reducing the noise level is a
waste of breath, if you ask me.

⚓ From the notion that a horse, being a horse, will never understand or
appreciate the prayer to Amida Buddha.

⊶ *baji-tōfu* 馬耳東風

● 馬を鹿と言う *uma o shika to iu* "call a horse a deer"
call black white; try to pull the wool over *someone's* eyes

○ それじゃあ、馬を鹿と言うのと同じじゃないか。
Sore jā, uma o shika to iu no to onaji ja nai ka.
You're full of it. / Who are you trying to kid?

○ あの人は馬を鹿と言う性格だから部下に慕われないんだよ。
*Ano hito wa uma o shika to iu seikaku da kara buka ni shitaware-
nai n' da yo.*
He's the kind of guy who's got to have his own way, right or
wrong, so nobody really wants to work for him.

○ お前のその馬を鹿と言う性格は誰に似たんだ。
Omae no sono uma o shika to iu seikaku wa dare ni nita n' da.
Which side of the family did you get that contrariness from?

⚓ Used to describe intentional misrepresentation of something or to say
something that flies in the face of facts for one's own purposes.

● 出馬（する）　*shutsuba (suru)*　"entering a horse"
run (stand) for (election/office)

○ 沢田さんは今度の選挙の出馬を決意した。
Sawada-san wa kondo no senkyo no shutsuba o ketsui shita.
Ms. Sawada made up her mind to run for office in the next election.

○ あの議員は今度出馬してもチャンスはないだろう。
Ano giin wa kondo shutsuba shite mo chansu wa nai darō.
Even if that representative runs in the next election, he doesn't stand much of a chance.

🐾 From the former practice of high-ranking warriors going to battle on horseback.

● 尻馬に乗る　*shiriuma ni noru*　"ride on the rear of a horse"
ride in on *someone's* coattails; jump on the bandwagon; go along uncritically with *something*

○ あんな奴の尻馬に乗るな。
Anna yatsu no shiriuma ni noru na.
I wouldn't go along with him (what he says) if I were you.

○ あいつの尻馬に乗ってそんな壺につぎ込んでいると身の破滅だぞ。
Aitsu no shiriuma ni notte sonna tsubo ni tsugikonde iru to mi no hametsu da zo.
You'll end up signing your own death warrant if you believe everything he tells you. / Jump on that bandwagon, and it'll lead to your downfall.

○ あの人の尻馬に付くような言動を続けていると、誰にも相手にされなくなるよ。
Ano hito no shiriuma ni tsuku yō na gendō o tsuzukete iru to, dare ni mo aite ni sarenaku naru yo.
If you keep following him around blindly like you are, nobody's going to pay any attention to you any more.

🐾 Originally *shiriuma* meant the rear of a horse with mounted rider, and then, by extension, to ride on the back of a horse behind someone else, i.e., ride on the horse's rump, as opposed to its back; hence, to go along with something or someone without exercising control of the direction events take or adhering to specific principles.

● 対抗馬　*taikōba*　"an opposing horse"
　a strong opponent, a contender, *someone* (usually a candidate) who will give *someone* a run for his/her money

○ 次期首相の本命の対抗馬として3人が出馬を表明した。
　Jiki-shushō no honmei no taikōba toshite sannin ga shutsuba o hyōmei shita.
　Three strong candidates threw their hats in the ring to oppose the frontrunner for the prime ministership.

○ あいつは対抗馬としてはたいしたことないな。
　Aitsu wa taikōba toshite wa taishita koto nai na.
　I'm not gonna lose any sleep over running against somebody like him.

🐎 From horse racing, of a horse considered capable of giving the favorite a run for the money, *taikōba* is now widely used in the political arena as well.

● 竹馬の友　*chikuba no tomo*　"stilt friends"
　a childhood friend, a friend from childhood

○ 竹馬の友は何年会ってなくても不思議と話がはずむ。
　Chikuba no tomo wa nannen atte 'nakute mo fushigi to hanashi ga hazumu.
　It's really weird how you can get together with a childhood friend after years and still find plenty to talk about.

🐎 The word for stilts originally meant a branch of bamboo, with the attached leaves bringing up the rear, ridden around like a horse by children. Later it was used to describe the tall poles (made of bamboo in Japan) with places to put your feet that provide children with a new perspective on life as well as yet another opportunity to injure themselves. As an independent word, 竹馬 is read *takeuma*.

● 付け馬　*tsukeuma*　"an attached horse"
　1. a person who goes home from a bar or cabaret with a customer to collect money he owes, a collector, enforcer

○ 付け馬をつけるとは、あの店もやるねえ。
　Tsukeuma o tsukeru to wa, ano mise mo yaru nē.
　That place has got some nerve. Imagine sending someone home with a customer to put the squeeze on him.

○ あの人は一度飲み始めると付け馬を引くほど飲む。
Ano hito wa ichido nomihajimeru to tsukeuma o hiku hodo nomu.
That guy starts drinking and it never fails; he's always got to go
home with some guy from the bar to get the money to pay up.

○ 今どき付け馬を連れて帰る人など山田さん以外いないな。
*Imadoki tsukeuma o tsurete kaeru hito nado Yamada-san igai inai
na.*
Yamada's the only guy I know who still gets followed home from
bars by dunners.

✌ From the practice of sending someone home with a patron to collect
the money for his bar or brothel bill. Based on its reported relation to
umatsunagi 馬繋ぎ, "hitching post," or the act of tying up a horse to such
an object, we may speculate that use of the expression derives from such
tethering of a horse in order to prevent it from wandering away. Hence,
although it remains unclear whether it is from the patron tethered to the
collector (*tsukeuma o tsukeru* or *hiku*) or from the collector tethered to
the drinking establishment (*tsukeuma*) that the idiom arises, its origin is
clearly to be found in keeping a horse tied up.

---

2. (criminal argot) a (police) tail

○ おまえ付け馬されてるぞ。
Omae tsukeuma sarete 'ru zo.
You're being tailed, man.

● とん馬 *tonma* "a stupid horse"
(of a person) an ass, airhead, idiot, a complete fool, zero,
nitwit; (of what such a person does or says) stupidity, fool-
ishness

○ 財布を忘れるなんてとん馬だなあ。
Saifu o wasureru nante tonma da nā.
What a dumbfuck, losing your wallet like that.

○ 入社式の日から遅刻するとはとん馬なやつだよ。
Nyūsha-shiki no hi kara chikoku suru to wa tonma na yatsu da yo.
Guy's got to be a certified zero to start a new job by arriving late
to the welcoming ceremony for new employees.

✌ No evidence that this expression ever meant "a stupid horse."

● 馬脚を露す *bakyaku o arawasu* "expose the horse's legs"

give *oneself* away, show *one's* true colors, reveal *one's* true
character, betray *oneself*, reveal *one's* cloven foot (hoof)

○ あいつ善人ぶっているがいつか馬脚を露すぞ。

Aitsu zennin butte iru ga itsuka bakyaku o arawasu zo.

He's faking being a nice guy. Give him some time and he'll give
himself away.

○ 彼はとうとう馬脚を露し、麻薬密売に手を染め始めた。

*Kare wa tōtō bakyaku o arawashi, mayaku-mitsubai ni te o some-
hajimeta.*

Eventually he showed his true colors by beginning to sell drugs.

⚜ From the stage, *bakyaku* —literally "horse's legs"—meant the person
dressed in a horse suit playing the role of the legs. For it to become ap-
parent through some mishap or otherwise that the horse was really
played by actors was to "expose the horse's legs," and later, by extension, to inadvertently reveal something one had attempted to conceal.

● 馬耳東風　*baji-tōfū*　"horse's ears, the east wind"

have no effect, (like) water off a duck's back; go in one ear
and out the other

○ 仕事に熱中している彼女に縁談の話をしても今は馬耳東風だな。

*Shigoto ni netchū shite iru kanojo ni endan no hanashi o shite mo
ima wa baji-tōfū da na.*

She's so wrapped up in her work right now that if you try to talk to
her about marriage, it just goes in one ear and out the other.

○ TVゲームに夢中になっている人間に何を言っても馬耳東風だ。

*Terebi gēmu ni muchū ni natte iru ningen ni nani o itte mo baji-
tōfū da.*

You might as well go talk to the wall as to someone engrossed in
playing Nintendo.

⚜ From the notion that a horse does not feel an easterly blowing in its ear.

↝ *uma no mimi ni nenbutsu* 馬の耳に念仏

● 馬車馬　*bashauma*　"a carriage horse"

a workhorse, a hard worker

○ 彼は死ぬまで馬車馬のように働き続けた。

Kare wa shinu made bashauma no yō ni hatarakitsuzuketa.

He worked like a dog until his dying day.

○ 彼、馬車馬のように働いてるけど、一体いつ寝ているんだ？

Kare, bashauma no yō ni hataraite 'ru kedo, ittai itsu nete 'ru n' da?

Wonder when a guy who works like a horse (slaves away) like he does ever gets any sleep?

🐾 From the way a carriage horse wearing blinders goes about its job singlemindedly. The idiom commonly appears followed by *no yō ni hataraku* .

● 馬子にも衣装　*mago ni mo ishō*　"clothes for even a driver" (the) clothes make the man

---

○ 馬子にも衣装っていうけど、本当に良く似合ってるよその服。

Mago ni mo ishō tte iu kedo, hontō ni yoku niatte 'ru yo sono fuku.

I know what they say about the clothes making the man, but you *really* look good in those duds.

○ スーツ新調して卒業パーティーに出たら、「馬子にも衣装」とからかわれた。

Sūtsu shinchō shite sotsugyō pātī ni detara, "mago ni mo ishō" to karakawareta.

I got teased about clothes making the man when I went to our graduation party in a new suit.

🐾 Commonly used in Japan as a modest response to praise or jocularly among friends.

● やじ（野次）馬　*yajiuma*　"a heckling horse" a rubberneck, gawker, curious bystander (onlooker)

○ その火事現場の周りは野次馬でいっぱいだった。

Sono kaji-genba no mawari wa yajiuma de ippai datta.

Curious bystanders were all around the scene of the fire.

○ 野次馬のせいで救急車の到着が遅れた。

Yajiuma no sei de kyūkyūsha no tōchaku ga okureta.

The ambulance was delayed by rubberneckers.

🐾 Possibly from the original meaning of "a difficult horse to break" or, according to one theory, from a shortening of *oyajiuma,* or "an old male horse," *oyaji* meaning old man. Although the word *yaji* means heckling, as in *yaji o tobasu* ヤジを飛ばす, a *yajiuma* is not a heckler. Confusing but true.

おおかみ（狼）　*ōkami*　wolf

☞ Now considered extinct, the last known *Nihon Ōkami* was shot and killed in 1905. And, no, public opinion is not divided by government plans to reintroduce these widely misunderstood canine carnivores into the nation's national parks. There are no such plans, not yet at least.

It was previously believed that the wolf was a divine creature capable of protecting humans from a variety of misfortunes. Folk practices related to this belief included use of a wolf's skull to guard from a form of mental illness known as fox possession, possibly from the fact that the wolf was a natural enemy of the fox.

Folk beliefs evoking wolves are often related to childbirth, since the mountain god, whom some folk tales depict as changing into a wolf, was also held to be the guardian god of childbirth.

In addition, the indigenous people of Japan's northernmost island Hokkaido, the Ainu, worshiped wolves and claim one as the father of the clan.

The wolf's howl is *uō-uō*. Wolves are counted *ippiki* 一匹 or *ittō* 一頭.

● 一匹狼　*ippiki ōkami*　"a single wolf"
  a lone wolf, loner, maverick

○ 彼は出版業界の一匹狼で通っている。
  Kare wa shuppan-gyōkai no ippiki ōkami de tōtte iru.
  He's known in the publishing industry as a maverick.

○ 一匹狼だったその男の居所を知る者はいない。
  Ippiki ōkami datta sono otoko no idokoro o shiru mono wa inai.
  Nobody knows the whereabouts of that loner.

● 狼少年　*ōkami shōnen*　"a wolf-boy"
  the boy who cried wolf (once too often); a habitual liar

○ そんないい加減なこと言ってると、狼少年になっちゃうよ。
  Sonna ii kagen na koto itte 'ru to, ōkami shōnen ni natchau yo.
  Nobody's going to believe you anymore if you keep crying wolf (bullshiting) all the time.

○ ダメだよ、あんな奴のこと信じちゃ、狼少年ってみんなに言われてるんだから。
  Dame da yo, anna yatsu no koto shinjicha, ōkami shōnen tte minna ni iwarete 'ru n' da kara.
  You can't believe that dude. Everyone says he's full of it (full of hot air, beans).

🦡 From *Aesop's Fables*.

● 送り狼 *okuri ōkami* "a see-you-home wolf"

a man professing to be a gentleman who escorts his date to her home, only to try to force her to have sex with him once he's in the door

---

○「彼ったら、『京子さん、ぼくがアパートまで送って行きましょう』って言うのよ。」

"Kare ttara 'Kyoko-san, boku ga apāto made okutte ikimashō' tte iu no yo."

"Then he ups and says, 'Kyoko, can I give you a lift home?'"

「せいぜい送り狼には気をつけてね。」

"Seizei okuri ōkami ni wa ki o tsukete ne."

"I'd watch out if I were you. He may not be as innocent as he seems."

○ 酒に弱い宏君は送り狼になるどころか、女友達に家まで送ってもらうことの方が多い。

Sake ni yowai Hiroshi-kun wa okuri ōkami ni naru dokoro ka, onna tomodachi ni ie made okutte morau koto no hō ga ōi.

Far from being a wolf on the prowl, Hiroshi usually ends up having to get a lift home with one of his girlfriends because he's so drunk.

🦡 From a former belief that there were wolves in Japan who followed travelers along lonely mountain roads either to protect them from other roving packs of wolves or attack them should the travelers ever look back to see if they were being followed (or stumble and fall, according to other versions).

きつね（狐） *kitsune* fox

☞ The fox, like the badger, was formerly believed capable of assuming many shapes as well as causing other things to change appearance in order to startle, deceive, or beguile humans. One popular folk tale has the guileful fox inviting a man out for a walk on a country road, where it then proceeds to deceive him by showing him a leaf that it has transformed into a gold coin. English words evoking foxes, like the verbs "fox" or "outfox," conjure up similar devious characteristics.

In a tale which shows possible, if distant linguistic similarities to the English use of fox to describe a sexually attractive young woman, a fox takes the shape of a beautiful woman to marry a man. Positive linguistic parallels pretty much end there, for in Japan these wily creatures rarely come off well in idiomatic usage. *Megitsune,* written with the characters for woman 女 and fox 狐, for example, is closer to bitch or vixen in English than to fox. Still, the identification of these secretive carnivores with cunning and craftiness in both languages indicates an astounding commonality of experience and imagination.

Foxes were also believed capable of possessing human beings, a notion that no doubt led to expressions like *kitsune ni tsumamareru,* which is included here.

In an interesting aside, there is even a word in Japanese, written (infrequently) with the characters for fox and odor 狐臭, that means tragomaschalia—"B.O." for most of us—and a "disease" in Japan. Fortunately, there is no evidence that it is carried or spread by our foxy friends, though ancient Japanese appear to have noticed that foxes do have a distinct, strong odor.

The fox's bark in Japanese is *konkon* コンコン. It is counted *ippiki* 一匹 or *ittō* 一頭.

● きつねそば（うどん）　*kitsune soba (udon)*　"fox *soba (udon)*"

buckwheat (wheat) noodles in broth and topped with a piece of fried tofu

---

○ きつねそばひとつください。

Kitsune soba hitotsu kudasai.

I'll take the kitsune soba.

○ 週に1回はきつねうどんを食べないと気がすまない。

Shū ni ikkai wa kitsune udon o tabenai to ki ga sumanai.

I don't feel right unless I eat *kitsune udon* at least once a week.

🦊 No, Japanese don't eat fox. These noodles derive their name from the belief that foxes like fried tofu, a belief borne out by the fact that the stylized guardian foxes known as *inari* bracing the *torii* of Shinto shrines are often presented with fried tofu offerings.

● 狐と狸の化かし合い　*kitsune to tanuki no bakashiai*　"the fox and the badger trying to outsmart each other"

try to outfox (outsmart) each other

○ 冷戦時代の米ソのスパイ活動は狐と狸の化かし合いであった。

Reisen-jidai no Bei-So no supai katsudō wa kitsune to tanuki no bakashiai de atta.

U.S. and Soviet spy operations during the Cold War were a constant game of one-upsmanship (cat and mouse).

○ そのライバル会社の商戦は、狐と狸の化かし合いで、もう何年も
  続いている。

*Sono raibaru-gaisha no shōsen wa, kitsune to tanuki no bakashiai
de, mō nannen mo tsuzuite iru.*

Those two rival companies have been trying to outsmart each
other for years.

✌ Both the fox and badger were formerly thought to be masters of deception, a belief that found its way into the language in this idiom, which
now enjoys wide use.

● 狐につままれる   *kitsune ni tsumamareru*   "be bewitched
by a fox"
be baffled, befuddled, foxed, puzzled, mystified; be at a loss

---

○ 1,000万円の賞金とは狐につままれたような話だ。

*Issenman-en no shōkin to wa kitsune ni tsumamareta yō na
hanashi da.*

Winning a ten million yen prize is just too good to be true.

○ 君のような美人が僕とつき合ってくれるなんて、なんだか狐につ
  ままれたような話だな。

*Kimi no yō na bijin ga boku to tsukiatte kureru nante, nan da ka
kitsune ni tsumamareta yō na hanashi da na.*

It's really baffling why a beautiful girl like you would go out with
me.

○ たった1時間道端に立っただけでこんな報酬になるなんてきっと
  狐につままれているにちがいない。

*Tatta ichiji-kan michibata ni tatta dake de konna hōshu ni naru
nante kitto kitsune ni tsumamarete iru ni chigai nai.*

There's something funny going on here! I can't believe that I could
earn this much money just standing by the road for an hour.

✌ From the belief that the fox can change its appearance to deceive humans comes this metaphoric use when something unbelievable occurs.

● 狐の嫁入り   *kitsune no yomeiri*   "a fox becomes a bride"
1. a sudden shower when the sun is shining, a sun shower

○ なんだ？狐の嫁入りか？

Nan da? Kitsune no yomeiri ka?

What's this? A sun shower?

○ 晴れているのに雨が……まるで狐の嫁入りだね。

Harete iru no ni ame ga ... maru de kitsune no yomeiri da ne.
Raining even though the sun is out ... just like a sun shower.

---

2. (from its resemblance to a procession of lanterns formerly carried at a wedding procession) a large number of will-o'-the-wisps or foxfires

---

○ 子供の頃おばあちゃんから裏山で狐の嫁入りを見たと聞かされ怖かった。

Kodomo no koro obāchan kara urayama de kitsune no yomeiri o mita to kikasare kowakatta.

I remember being scared when I was little and my grandma told me about seeing will-o'-the-wisps deep in the mountains.

● 狐火 *kitsunebi* "a fox fire"
a foxfire; a will-o'-the-wisp, an ignis fatuus, a jack-o'-lantern

○ あの山はよく狐火が見えるらしい。
Ano yama wa yoku kitsunebi ga mieru rashii.
They say that you can see a lot of foxfires on that mountain.

○ 子供たちはその山の狐火の話を聞いて怖くなった。
Kodomo-tachi wa sono yama no kitsunebi no hanashi o kiite kowaku natta.
The children got scared when they heard stories of the foxfires on the mountain.

🐾 From the old belief that foxes breathed fire. There are also folk tales of foxes carrying lanterns in their own version of a wedding procession. Also called *onibi* 鬼火, or ogre fire.

● 狐目 *kitsuneme* "fox's eyes"
thin, sharp eyes

○ この狐目の男に見覚えはありませんか？
Kono kitsuneme no otoko ni mioboe wa arimasen ka?
Do you remember ever seeing this man with thin eyes before?

○ 眼鏡をかけてるから気がつかないけど、彼女どっちかというと狐目してるよね。
Megane o kakete 'ru kara ki ga tsukanai kedo, kanojo dotchi ka to iu to kitsuneme shite 'ru yo ne.
It's hard to tell when she's wearing glasses, but her eyes are kind of thin.

🐾 Not, by Japanese standards of physical beauty, the kind of eyes you want to have.

● 古狐 *furugitsune* "an old fox"
a sly old bitch, a wily old bat, a cunning old battleax, a grimalkin

---

○ あの古狐め、いつか思い知らせてやる。
Ano furugitsune-me, itsuka omoishirasete yaru.
I'll show the old witch some day.

○ 古狐と呼ばれていた彼女もいまではその面影もなくひっそりと暮らしている。
Furugitsune to yobarete ita kanojo mo ima de wa sono omokage mo naku hissori to kurashite iru.
Everybody used to call her a wily old bat, but you sure couldn't tell from how quietly she's living now.

🐾 Used almost exclusively of women.

↪ *furudanuki* 古狸 (of men)

● 牝狐 *megitsune* "a vixen"
a bitch, witch; a shrew, vixen

○ あの牝狐め、色仕掛けで秘密を探り出そうとしている。
Ano megitsune-me, irojikake de himitsu o saguridasō to shite iru.
That bitch is batting her eyelashes around trying to find out what's going on.

○ あの牝狐に引っかかったらどんな男もダメになる。
Ano megitsune ni hikkakattara donna otoko mo dame ni naru.
I don't care who you are, let that witch get her claws in you and that's all she wrote (you're done for).

🐾 From the belief that foxes take the form of a woman to deceive people. Appears almost exclusively preceded by *ano*.

熊 *kuma* bear

☞ As conspicuous by their absence from the language as from the land, bears are seldom seen in Japan although distant cousins of the grizzlies do roam parts of Hokkaido, and an occasional black bear is shot for sport or because it has wandered innocently into some inhabited area—which is to say it has shown its face where some hunter "loaded for bear" could get a clean shot at it. Because there are no idioms regarding bears to be found, a necessarily brief discussion of a couple of metaphoric senses of the noun itself and one or two nouns with ursine elements will have to suffice. First, what it is not in Japanese: it is neither a downward-trending market nor a pessimist who sees such a market in the offing. Nor is it a surly person, difficult problem, or class of students in the party mode.

That having been said, the character is prefixed to a number of nouns, usually other fauna or flora, to indicate largeness, viciousness, or fearfulness. There are "bear" cicadas, bees, hawks, and rats, all larger and more fearful than other species of the same kind; there are even killer strawberries, *kumaichigo* 熊苺, or "bear" strawberries. And then there is the *kumade* 熊手, or "bear paw," a rake so named from the similarity of the scratches it leaves to those left by a bear's paw. *Kumade* can also be used metaphorically to signify greed, as in *kumadeshō* 熊手性, or an avaricious nature and, perhaps, ham-handedness or uncouthness, as in *kumadebaba* 熊手婆, a now seldom-heard expression of disdain for a grabby old woman or a coarse midwife who all but rakes fetuses out of the womb. Were abortion a moral problem in Japan, this term would no doubt have already been appropriated by Oriental right-to-lifers.

In the bygone days of Japanese theater, the gallery was separated from the more expensive seats by iron bars, presumably to prevent the rabble from mixing with their snooty brothers and sisters. Viewed from outside, those in this Japanese version of "nigger heaven" were seen to be behind bars in a cage like bears, hence the name *kuma* was used of those standing in the peanut gallery at dramatic performances. The few bears that remain to shit in the Japanese woods are counted *ippiki* 一匹 or *ittō* 一頭. You probably won't ever have to count more than that.

こうもり（蝙蝠）　*kōmori*　bat

☞　Although there are some twenty-five species of bats that can be found in Japan, this much maligned nocturnal mammal figures in but one idiom and a single picturesque description of an umbrella, now seldom seen. Shunned as much for their facial resemblance to rats as any imagined notion of nefariousness, bats can still be observed intercepting insects in midair in the night skies in certain areas of Tokyo.

Bats are counted *ippiki* 一匹 or *ichiwa* 一羽.

● こうもり傘　*kōmorigasa*　"a bat umbrella"
a big black umbrella

○ 最近ではこうもり傘を見かけなくなった。
Saikin de wa kōmorigasa o mikakenaku natta.
You don't see many big, black umbrellas around anymore.

○ 当時の私の祖父はこうもり傘に黒マントというういでだちで町を歩
いていたそうです。

Tōji no watashi no sofu wa kōmorigasa ni kuro-manto to iu idedachi de machi o aruite ita sō desu.

In those days my grandfather used to walk around in a cape and carry a big black umbrella.

✌ Also called just *kōmori,* these Western-style umbrellas, as opposed to traditional bamboo and paper Japanese umbrellas called *bangasa* 番傘, appear to be on the endangered list. Before umbrellas became fashion statements, most were black and, whether opened to expose the ribs underneath that appeared to resemble the wings of a bat when viewed from below, or folded as a bat might fold its wings, the umbrella evoked the image of a bat strongly enough to warrant its name. With the gradual decline of all-black umbrellas, the word is heard less and less today, although older Japanese still use it.

さる（猿）　*saru*　monkey

☞ Where would these little primates be if it weren't for Charles Darwin? Not in the schools as living proof that we too once had prehensile tails and funny looking butts, that's for sure. They suffer by comparison to humans, a relief to those of us who need to know we're not at the bottom of the heap, and although they figure in several idioms touting intelligence, Japanese monkeys never quite measure up to human standards and usually end up with the short end of the stick in folktales. In general, they are considered to be resourceful, quick, fidgety, and, yes, stupid.

The monkey's cry is *kīkī* キーキー or *kya'-kya'* キャッキャッ. They are counted *ippiki* 一匹 or *ittō* 一頭. Written 申, the monkey is the ninth of the twelve signs of the Chinese zodiac.

● 猿ぐつわ　*sarugutsuwa*　"a monkey bit"
a gag

○ 猿ぐつわをかまされていたので助けを呼ぶことが出来なかった。

Sarugutsuwa o kamasarete ita no de tasuke o yobu koto ga dekinakatta.

I couldn't call out for help, because they had me gagged.

○ 目隠しと猿ぐつわをされていたので、どこをどうやって連れてこ
られたのかかいもく見当がつかない。

Mekakushi to sarugutsuwa o sarete ita no de, doko o dō yatte tsurete korareta no ka kaimoku kentō ga tsukanai.

I don't have the slightest idea where they took me because I was gagged and blindfolded.

🐒 From the fact that *saru* is the name of a small, usually wooden, sliding block used to lock shutters from the inside. The connection between the animal and the sliding block is unclear. The connection between the sliding block that slides into a hole in the window, door frame, or lintel (which, by the way, is a "duck place" 鴨居 another story) and the expression *sarugutsuwa* is clearer, the point being to stuff a hole—one's mouth, for example—with something.

● 猿芝居 *sarushibai* "a monkey (mime) show"
1. (of a dramatic production) a bad play, a joke

○ この前小さな劇団の公演見たけど、猿芝居もいいとこだったよ。
Kono mae chiisana gekidan no kōen mita kedo, sarushibai mo ii toko datta yo.
The other day I went to a play put on by a small troupe, but it was really amateurish.

---

2. (of extremely stupid behavior or a transparent scheme or plot) monkey business, a sham, mumbo jumbo

---

○ へたな猿芝居はやめろ。
Heta na sarushibai wa yamero.
Cut out the mumbo jumbo, man.

○ そんな猿芝居すぐばれてしまうぞ。
Sonna sarushibai sugu barete shimau zo.
You're not fooling anyone with that monkey business.

🐒 From this rudimental form of entertainment in which a trained monkey is made to act out a play, this idiom is used to describe a poorly produced play or some shallow, ill-conceived deception or otherwise ridiculous behavior.

● 猿知恵 *sarujie* "monkey wisdom"
shallow cunning

○ 猿知恵のはたらく奴だな、お前は。
Sarujie no hataraku yatsu da na, omae wa.
You may think you're smart, but you're not.

○ そんな猿知恵すぐ見破られるぞ。
Sonna sarujie sugu miyaburareru zo.
They're gonna see right through an asinine stunt like that.

🐒 Monkeys have long been compared with humans. One popular ancient belief appears to have been that they were just three hairs short of being human, *saru wa ningen yori ke ga sanbon tarinai* 猿は人間より毛が三本足りない. The expression can be used to convey the belief that monkeys fall slightly short of human wisdom.

● 猿真似　*sarumane*　"monkey mimicking"
apery, copycatting, mimicry, mockery; monkey see, monkey do; a copy, fake, crib, knock off

---

○ この作品は単なる猿真似だ。
Kono sakuhin wa tan naru sarumane da.
The work is nothing more than a copy.

○ しょせん猿真似は猿真似。本物にはかなわない。
Shosen sarumane wa sarumane. Honmono ni wa kanawanai.
When it's all said and done, it's still just a fake. It's not even close to the original.

🐰 From the observation that monkeys often ape humans, and the happy discovery that they never quite pull it off.

● 猿も木から落ちる　*saru mo ki kara ochiru*　"even a monkey can fall out of a tree"
even Homer sometimes nods, anybody can make a mistake, nobody's perfect

---

○ 彼がそんな単純なミスを犯すなんて、猿も木から落ちるんだな。
Kare ga sonna tanjun na misu o okasu nante, saru mo ki kara ochiru n' da na.
For him to make such a simple mistake makes you realize that it can happen to the best of us.

○「猿も木から落ちる … か。」
"Saru mo ki kara ochiru ... ka."
"I guess nobody's perfect."

「え？」
"E?"
"Come again."

「あのF1ドライバー首都高でおかまほったらしいよ。」
"Ano F-1 doraibā shutokō de okama hotta rashii yo."
"It looks like that F-1 racer rammed into the back of some car on the Tokyo freeway."

● 見猿聞か猿言わ猿 *mizaru kikazaru iwazaru* "see monkey, hear monkey, speak monkey"
  see no evil, hear no evil, and speak no evil

○ こんな厄介なことごめんだ、見猿聞か猿言わ猿でいこう。
  Konna yakkai na koto gomen da, mizaru kikazaru iwazaru de ikō.
  I don't want to have anything to do with this hassle; I'm just gonna keep my distance.

○ 夫婦の問題にお節介は禁物だよ、こういうことは見猿聞か猿言わ猿が一番いいんだよ。
  Fūfu no mondai ni osekkai wa kinmotsu da yo, kō iu koto wa mizaru kikazaru iwazaru ga ichiban ii n' da yo.
  You've got to stay away from domestic quarrels like the plague. The best policy is just not to see anything, hear anything, or say anything.

🐵 Yeah, it *is* the same three monkeys we've all seen somewhere advising us, by covering their eyes, ears and mouth, to butt out of other people's business and to protect our own interests. The ~*zaru* ～猿 is a play on the homonymic Japanese negative-verb ending ~*zaru* ～ざる. Hence, *mizaru* means "not see," etc.

● 山猿 *yamazaru* "a mountain monkey"
  a rustic; a clodhopper, a boor

○ あんな山猿に会社を乗っ取られてたまるもんか。
  Anna yamazaru ni kaisha o nottorarete tamaru mon ka.
  If you think I'm going to stand by while some hick takes over the company, you've got another think coming.

○ 若い頃は山猿と馬鹿にされていた彼も、今では売れっ子の詩人になった。
  Wakai koro wa yamazaru to baka ni sarete ita kare mo, ima de wa ureko no shijin ni natta.
  Once treated like a country bumpkin, he's a best-selling poet now.

🐵 The original meaning is a wild mountain monkey. No surprises there, huh. Metaphorically it became a derisive term for an unschooled person from the country, untutored in the niceties of urban life.

たぬき（狸）　　*tanuki*　raccoon dog

☞ When found in idioms describing people, this is basically the male equivalent of *kitsune,* or fox, which is used primarily of women. Both animals were thought capable of bewitching humans. The raccoon dog has large, round eyes, which make it, unlike the fox, a lovable creature. But the *tanuki* was also believed to possess humans, making their appetites become uncontrollable and their stomachs distend as they grew listless and weak and eventually died. *Tanuki* are the animals immortalized in porcelain outside many Japanese taverns and pubs. Characteristically, they have scrotums about half the size of their diminutive bodies, about which ditties have been written and idioms created. According to one such idiom, the *tanuki*'s scrotum spreads out over eight tatami mats (*tanuki no kintama hachi-jō jiki* 狸のきん玉八畳敷).

Tanuki are counted *ippiki* 一匹. They are too small to warrant being counted *ittō* 一頭.

● 狸　*tanuki*　"raccoon dog"
　　a cunning person, sly (crafty) fellow, an old fox (coon); no-
　　body's fool

○ あの人はなかなかの狸だよね。
　Ano hito wa nakanaka no tanuki da yo ne.
　That guy's crazy (dumb) like a fox. / There're no flies on him. /
　He's a foxy (cagey) fellow.

○ 政治家なんて狸じゃなきゃやってけないよ。
　Seiji-ka nante tanuki ja nakya yatte 'ke nai yo.
　You've got to be wily (crafty) to make it as a politician.

○ 相手は相当な狸おやじだから気をつけろよ。
　Aite wa sōto na tanuki oyaji da kara ki o tsukero yo.
　Better watch yourself, the guy you'll be dealing with is an old
　sharpie.

🦡 Used primarily of men on the distant side of forty. When followed by *oyaji* it is reserved exclusively for males. Although rarely, *tanuki* can be used of both sexes. As the examples indicate, by convention the expression is often preceded by a qualifer like *sōto na* or *nakanaka no.*

● たぬき寝入り　*tanuki-neiri*　"a raccoon dog sleeping"
　　playing possum, pretending to be asleep

○ 彼は分が悪くなったのでたぬき寝入りを決め込んだ。
　Kare wa bu ga waruku natta no de tanuki-neiri o kimekonda.
　He made up his mind to play possum when things started going
　against him.

○ ちょっと、たぬき寝入りなんかしないで、私の話を聞いてよ。

Chotto, tanuki-neiri nanka shinai de, watashi no hanashi o kiite yo.
Come on now, don't pretend to be asleep. Listen to what I'm saying.

○ 席をゆずるのが面倒だから、電車ではたぬき寝入りをするという
　人がけっこういるよ。

*Seki o yuzuru no ga mendō da kara, densha de wa tanuki-neiri o
suru to iu hito ga kekkō iru yo.*

There are lots of people who don't want to give up their seats on
the train, so they pretend to be asleep.

🐾 Said to have its origin in the days when no distinction was made between the *tanuki* and the *mujina* 貉 or badger, and the latter was believed
to have been unable to see or hear during the daytime and therefore
likely to just sit tight and try not to attract too much attention to itself.
Today the most common place to find people playing possum is in
crowded commuter trains and subways, where younger people lucky
enough to have found seats feign sleep to avoid making eye contact with
elderly commuters to whom social convention dictates they give up their
seat. Along with both its less common variations, *tanuki* 狸 and *tanuki-ne*
狸寝, the idiom is not used—as it's English equivalent "play possum"
is—to mean "feign ignorance."

● 捕らぬ狸の皮算用　*toranu tanuki no kawazan'yō* "counting the pelts of untrapped raccoon dogs"
counting one's chickens before they hatch

○ 「この計算でいけば、10カ月で100万儲かるよ。」
"Kono keisan de ikeba, jukkagetsu de hyaku-man mōkaru yo."
"The way I've got it figured, we're gonna make a million yen in
ten months."

「捕らぬ狸の皮算用にならなければいいけど。」
"Toranu tanuki no kawazan'yō ni naranakereba ii kedo."
"Let's just hope we're not counting our chickens before they hatch."

○ あいつはいつも捕らぬ狸の皮算用ばかりで、言ったとおりになっ
　たことがない。

*Aitsu wa itsumo toranu tanuki no kawazan'yō bakari de, itta tōri
ni natta koto ga nai.*

She's always counting her chickens before they hatch; nothing
ever turns out the way she says it will.

🐾 In addition to the usual explanation of overeagerness, another theory
regarding this idiom relates to the *tanuki*'s ability to possess a human. In
this somewhat farfetched view, the number of *tanuki* pelts actually taken
differs from the count because the wily animal has somehow deceived
the trapper.

● 古狸　*furudanuki*　"an old raccoon dog"
a sly old fox, a wily (crafty) old dog

○ あの古狸また新入社員をいびってるらしいぞ。
Ano furudanuki mata shinnyū-shain o ibitteru rashii zo.
That wily old dog is at it again, giving the new employees a hard time.

○ あの人は古狸だからうかつなこと言うな。
Ano hito wa furudanuki da kara ukatsu na koto iu na.
Watch what you say around him, he's a sly old fox.

  🦌 Used exclusively of older men.

  ∞ *furugitsune* 古狐 (of older women)

とら（虎）　*tora*　tiger

  ☞　The king of beasts to most Japanese, perhaps because unlike the African lion it is close to home; indigenous to neighboring China and Korea and figuring in numerous folk tales and stories in the region. Widely feared for its ferocity and fabled predilICtion for attacking humans, the tiger was targeted by Japanese who traveled to the then distant Korean peninsula to eradicate them. While tigers survived that onslaught, they have not fared so well in modern times as their habitat is gradually being destroyed by ever expanding Asian populations and economies.

  Tigers are counted any way they want to be, but *ippiki* 一匹 or *ittō* 一頭 are both safe.

  When used as the third sign of the Chinese zodiac, *tora* is written 寅.

● 虎穴に入らずんば虎児を得ず　*koketsu ni irazunba koji o ezu*　"you can't catch a tiger cub without going in the tiger's lair"
nothing ventured, nothing gained

○ 「虎穴に入らずんば虎児を得ず」だ、思い切って彼女に気持ちを打ち明けてみたら。
"Koketsu ni irazunba koji o ezu" da, omoikitte kanojo ni kimochi o uchiakete mitara.
You know what they say, nothing ventured, nothing gained. Why don't you just tell her how you feel about her?

○ 「虎穴に入らずんば虎子を得ず」、あのスラム街に潜入して情報収集するしかない。

"Koketsu ni irazunba koji o ezu," ano suramu-gai ni sennyū shite jōhō-shūshū suru shika nai.

Sometimes you've got to take risks. I guess there's no way around it, I've got to just go into the slum to get the info I need.

● 虎になる   *tora ni naru*   "become a tiger"
a bad (violent, uncontrollable) drunk; get Dutch [drunken] courage; get shitfaced, falling-down drunk, bombed, blotto, tanked, dead drunk, drunk as a skunk, potted, smashed, embalmed, pissed, bent, potted

---

○ あの人は飲むと虎になるから一緒に飲むのはやめたよ。

Ano hito wa nomu to tora ni naru kara issho ni nomu no wa yameta yo.

He gets a mean streak whenever he ties one on, so I quit drinking with him.

○ 昨日は久々に虎になったよ。

Kinō wa hisabisa ni tora ni natta yo.

I got wiped out yesterday for the first time in quite a while.

✌ The association of tigers and alcohol is from the figurative reference to alcohol as *chikuyō* 竹 葉 or *take no ha* 竹 の 葉 , literally "bamboo leaves," and the belief that tigers lurk in bamboo groves. The association of tigers with alcohol is not uniquely Japanese. In American slang, for example, cheap or inferior liquor is called tiger piss or tiger sweat, and a strong alcoholic drink is known as tiger juice.

● 虎の威を借る狐   *tora no i o karu kitsune*   "a fox borrowing the prestige of a lion"
an otherwise powerless person strutting about or throwing his weight around because of the power of the person he works for; an ass in a lion's skin; a nobody acting big because of his superior's power

---

○ あいつは社長の息子だと思って虎の威を借る狐になっているんだ。

Aitsu wa shachō no musuko da to omotte tora no i o karu kitsune ni natte iru n' da.

He thinks he can throw his weight around just because he's the president's son.

○ あんな虎の威を借る狐は相手にしなくて大丈夫だよ。

Anna tora no i o karu kitsune wa aite ni shinakute daijōbu da yo.

He's just acting big because he's got some guy upstairs behind him. You don't have to pay any attention to him.

● 虎の子　*tora no ko*　"tiger cub"
one's treasure; (of money) one's nest egg

○ 彼は虎の子の貯金をはたいたが事業に失敗した。
Kare wa tora no ko no chokin o hataita ga jigyō ni shippai shita.
He put up all his savings, but the business failed.

○ 全日本は虎の子の1点を守り切れず、引き分けてしまった。
Zen-Nippon wa tora no ko no itten o mamorikirezu, hikiwakete shimatta.
The All-Japan team couldn't hold on to its hard-earned one-point lead, and the game ended in a tie.

○ 彼女は長年かけて貯めた虎の子の金を男に騙し取られた。
Kanojo wa naganen kakete tameta tora no ko no kane o otoko ni damashitorareta.
She had the nest egg she'd saved up for years ripped off by some guy.

⚘ From the belief that a tiger takes very good care of its cubs. By convention this expression is used most commonly upon the loss of something treasured.

● 虎の巻　*tora no maki*　"a tiger-tome"
a crib, a pony, a study guide; a book of secret teachings

○ その虎の巻どこで手に入れたの。
Sono tora no maki doko de te ni ireta no.
Where'd you get ahold of that pony?

○ この虎の巻を使って勉強すれば試験はバッチリだ。
Kono tora no maki o tsukatte benkyō sureba shiken wa batchiri da.
With this crib, the test'll be a breeze.

○ この虎の巻さえあれば、鬼に金棒だ。
Kono tora no maki sae areba, oni ni kanabō da.
There'll be no stopping you with this pony in your arsenal.

○ これが伊賀忍者の虎の巻です。
Kore ga Iga-ninja no tora no maki desu.
This contains the secret teachings of the Iga ninja.

彡 From an ancient Chinese text expounding secret military strategies. As the last example illustrates, it also means a text that encapsulates the secrets of an artistic or martial tradition or its practices. In the sense of "crib" it is also called *torakan* 虎巻 or *anchoko* アンチョコ, the latter said to be a corruption of *anchoku* 安直, which in addition to meaning cheap or inexpensive, also means easy or simple.

ねこ（猫） *neko* cat

☞ Despite being one of the most common animals in and around human habitations—this is especially true of urban Japan, where clowders form at shrines in the early hours of evening to preen and perhaps boast of the day's adventures—and although they are held to be smart, cunning, and mysterious, cats failed to make the Chinese zodiac menagerie. According to one account, this is due to the fact that the cat alone among all animals did not show up at a meeting called by one of the gods. This handy anecodote also accounts for the reason why cats chase mice, for it was the mouse who is said to have wrongly informed the cat of the date for the meeting. Often appearing in Japanese ghost stories where they take the forms of monsters, cats were also believed to harm people.

In the early 1990s, cats figured in several short-lived idioms that burst on the linguistic scene only to all but disappear within a few years. *Nekobaba genshō* 猫ババ現象 (cats and grandmothers phenomenon), a homonym for *nekobaba* 猫ばば (an idiom included in this book), apparently started when some waggish door-to-door salesmen found no one home but cats (*neko*) and grandmothers (*baba*) when they came calling, Japanese housewives having discovered the joys of part-time work, health clubs, culture centers, lovers' trysts, and the freedom of two-income families.

A second linguistic flash in the pan in the nineties involving cats also illustrated the changing times. *Nekogata shain,* ネコ型社員 (cat-type employees) were singled out for criticism for their self-centeredness. These willful workers were said to launch enthusiastically into tasks they found interesting, but be almost catlike in their utter disinterest in anything else. Employers and social commentators alike bemoaned the changes in society that allowed a worker, heaven forbid, to have an opinion or an abiding interest in something beyond the corporate weal.

Not to be outdone by their canine competition, and perhaps hoping to reverse feline fortunes, Japanese cat lovers took a hint from some Belgian Festival and designated February 22, 1988, as the first Cat Day, or *Neko no Hi* 猫の日. The date was set by playing on the cat's meow, *nyā-nyā,* "two" being pronounced *ni*—hey, it's only a slight stretch—and the date having all those twos in it.

The cat's meow, literally, is *nyānyā* ニャーニャー. They are counted *ippiki* 一匹.

● 借りてきた猫　*karite kita neko*　"a borrowed cat"
be a pussycat; (uncharacteristically) quiet or well man-
nered; be lamblike

○ 花子は叔父さんの家に行くのが初めてだったので、借りてきた猫
のようだった。

*Hanako wa ojisan no ie ni iku no ga hajimete datta no de, karite
kita neko no yō datta.*

Hanako was uncharacteristically well behaved because it was the
first time she visited her uncle.

○ 毒舌の彼も奥さんの前では借りてきた猫だ。

Dokuzetsu no kare mo okusan no mae de wa karite kita neko da.

He's usually pretty poison-tongued, but he's a regular pussycat
around his wife.

🐾 One of my personal all-time favorites. From the observation that a cat
in unfamiliar surroundings, subdued and uncertain, appears well behaved. But put his rambunctious self on home turf and you've got a
horse of a different color, so to speak. Often followed by *no yō* or *mitai*.

● 鳴く猫（は）鼠をとらぬ　*naku neko (wa) nezumi o toranu*
"a meowing cat catches no rats"
talk a good show, (be) all talk, talk big but be unable to produce

---

○ 鳴く猫鼠をとらぬ、彼女は辞めないよ。

Naku neko nezumi o toranu, kanojo wa yamenai yo.

She's full of hot air. She's never going to quit her job.

○ 「鳴く猫は鼠をとらぬ」というが、あの人本当に事業始めるのか
なあ。

*"Naku neko wa nezumi o toranu" to iu ga, ano hito hontō ni jigyō
hajimeru no ka nā.*

The way he tends to be all talk and no action makes me wonder if
he'll ever go into business for himself.

● 猫かわいがりする　*neko-kawaigari suru*　"indulge a cat"
dote on

○ 山田さん夫婦は娘を猫かわいがりしている。

Yamada-san fūfu wa musume o neko-kawaigari shite iru.

The Yamadas really dote on their daughter.

○ 先生は、一番弟子の山本さんばかり猫かわいがりするので、ほかの弟子はやめていってしまう。

Sensei wa, ichiban-deshi no Yamamoto-san bakari neko-kawaigari suru no de, hoka no deshi wa yamete itte shimau.

The prof's always paying so much attention to Yamamoto, her favorite student, that the others stop coming.

🐾 This expression of extreme care and attention comes from the idea that cat lovers seem to think their cat is the cat's pajamas.

● 猫舌 *nekojita* "cat's tongue"
(a person who) can't eat or drink hot things

○ 私は猫舌です。
Watashi wa nekojita desu.
I don't like hot things.

○ これは猫舌の人にはすぐ食べられない料理かも知れない。
Kore wa nekojita no hito ni wa sugu taberarenai ryōri kamo shirenai.
This is probably too hot for you if you burn your tongue easily.

🐾 From the fact that cats are prone to throwing catfits when they try to lap up food or milk heated by well-meaning doters. This is what you've got if a layer of skin comes off the roof of your mouth when you try to get that hot coffee down. Many foreigners come off looking like they have a terminal case of cat's tongue when they eat ramen or udon without slurping it down and end up burning their tongue or throat. The secret is to suck a lot of air in with the noodles to cool them as they go down. It's your one chance in Japan to make noise when you're eating, without being scolded. Be aware, this expression can not be applied to those who do not like spicey foods.

● 猫背 *nekoze* "a cat's back"
a slight stoop, rounded shoulders

○ 本を読むときはもっと姿勢よくしなさい、猫背になっちゃうよ。
Hon o yomu toki wa motto shisei yoku shinasai, nekoze ni natchau yo.
Sit up straight (don't slouch) when you're reading or you'll end up having a stoop.

○ スキーの基本姿勢のこつは猫背を保つことです。
Sukī no kihon-shisei no kotsu wa nekoze o tamotsu koto desu.
The secret to the proper skiing position is to keep your shoulders hunched over.

🐾 From the similarity between such a posture and that of a cat when it has hunched up its back in a stretch or a threat. It is definitely not complimentary.

● 猫っ毛　*nekokke* "cat hair"
soft, fine hair [on one's head]

○ 私、猫っ毛なのよ。
Watashi, nekokke na no yo.
I've got fine hair.

○ 猫っ毛で薄いから、雨なんかに濡れると最悪よ。
Nekokke de usui kara, ame nanka ni nureru to saiaku yo.
I've got this thin, fine hair so it's the pits when it gets wet in the rain.

🐾 From the resemblance of such hair to a cat's soft fur.

● 猫撫で声　*nekonade-goe* "a cat-cajoling voice"
a coaxing (wheedling, flattering) (tone of) voice

○ 洋子は猫撫で声で母親にそのドレスをねだった。
Yōko wa nekonade-goe de haha-oya ni sono doresu o nedatta.
Yoko begged her mother in a coaxing voice to buy the dress.

○ 何だその猫撫で声は、今度は何が欲しいんだ？
Nan da sono nekonade-goe wa, kondo wa nani ga hoshii n' da?
What do you want now, talking sweet like that?

🐾 Studies, by the way, show that many cat lovers unconsciously raise their voice an octave or two when talking to their pets. Maybe there is something to this idiom besides fancy.

● 猫に鰹節（を預ける）　*neko ni katsuobushi (o azukeru)*
"entrusting a cat with a dried bonito"
trust a wolf to watch over sheep, leave a fox to guard the henhouse

○ 借金で首が回らなくなっている彼にそんな大金を預けるなんて、猫に鰹節を預けるようなものだ。
Shakkin de kubi ga mawaranaku natte iru kare ni sonna taikin o azukeru nante, neko ni katsuobushi o azukeru yō na mono da.
Entrusting a guy like that, up to his ears in debt, with all that money is asking for trouble.

o そんな学生の目の届くところに試験の原稿を置くなんて、猫に鰹節じゃないか。

Sonna gakusei no me no todoku tokoro ni shiken no genkō o oku nante, neko ni katsuobushi ja nai ka.

Don't you think you're inviting trouble by leaving the test questions lying around where students can see them?

● 猫に小判 *neko ni koban* "gold coins to a cat"
like casting pearls before swine

---

o そんな小さな子にコンピュータを買い与えるなんて、猫に小判だ。

Sonna chiisana ko ni konpyūta o kaiataeru nante, neko ni koban da.

Buying a computer for a small child like that is simply a waste.

o 彼にそんな高級なゴルフクラブは猫に小判だ。

Kare ni sonna kōkyū na gorufu-kurabu wa neko ni koban da.

A guy like that with expensive golf clubs! What a terrible waste!

From the fact that a cat cannot appreciate the value of a gold coin, *neko ni koban* expresses the futility of an unappreciative person possessing something of value. Seldom if ever used of abstractions, including ideas or emotions.

buta ni shinjū 豚に真珠, *uma no mimi ni nenbutsu* 馬（の耳）に念仏

● 猫にまたたび *neko ni matatabi* "catnip to a cat"
sure to produce the desired effect; a cure all

---

o 猫にまたたび、うちの子供にはテレビゲーム。

Neko ni matatabi, uchi no kodomo ni wa terebi-gēmu.

Turning my kids loose with a Nintendo will do the trick every time.

o うちの亭主は酒の肴にピーナッツを出しておけば猫にまたたびだから楽よ。

Uchi no teishu wa sake no sakana ni pīnattsu o dashite okeba neko ni matatabi da kara raku yo.

All you have to do is give my husband his sake and some peanuts, and he gets quiet as a mouse.

● 猫の子一匹いない *neko no ko ippiki inai* "not even a kitten around"
abandoned, no sign of life

○ 警察が現場に到着したときには猫の子一匹いなかった。

Keisatsu ga genba ni tōchaku shita toki ni wa neko no ko ippiki inakatta.

There wasn't a soul around when the police arrived at the scene.

○ こんな猫の子一匹いない場所に呼び出して、いったい何の用だ？

Konna neko no ko ippiki inai basho ni yobidashite, ittai nan no yō da?

What do you want with me out here in the middle of nowhere?

𝔰 From the observation that cats have lots of kittens. The reasoning is that if there isn't even a kitten around, the place must really be forlorn. Always in the negative, *neko no ko ippiki inai* is used of a place where there are no signs of life.

● 猫の手も借りたい　*neko no te mo karitai*　"want to borrow a cat's paw"

(be) swamped, overloaded, up to one's ass (in work), be short-handed

---

○ 今日は猫の手も借りたいほど忙しい。

Kyō wa neko no te mo karitai hodo isogashii.

We're up to our ass in work today. / We're busier than a bunch of one-armed paperhangers today.

○ 店は猫の手も借りたいほどなのに、お前は遊びに行くつもりなのか。

Mise wa neko no te mo karitai hodo na no ni, omae wa asobi ni iku tsumori na no ka.

We need every warm body we can get at the shop, and you think you're going out?

𝔰 Unlike dogs, cats are a notoriously good-for-nothing bunch in Japan. This idiom expresses just how close the speaker is to scraping the bottom of the barrel for help. *Mo* often replaces *o*, and *hodo* or *gurai* follows the whole to emphasize how busy one is.

● 猫の額（程の）　*neko no hitai (hodo no)*　"(about as big as) a cat's forehead"

a tiny plot of land, postage stamp-size piece of ground; a hole in the wall, cubbyhole

---

○ 東京では、猫の額ほどの土地が何千万円もする。

Tokyo de wa, neko no hitai hodo no tochi ga nanzenman-en mo suru.

A piece of ground so small you can't even swing a cat can cost tens of millions of yen in Tokyo.

○ その居酒屋は猫の額ほどの広さで、細々と商売している。

Sono izakaya wa neko no hitai hodo no hirosa de, hosoboso to shōbai shite iru.

That hole-in-the-wall tavern is just scraping by.

෴ Quick, find a cat and check out its forehead. If you can find it, that is. It's about the same situation with space in Japan, there's just not a lot of it to go around. Although this colorful expression is most commonly used about land, as the second example illustrates it may also be used to describe a small indoor space as well. It is commonly followed by *hodo no*. Though rare, there is also a shortened form, *nekobitai* 猫額.

● 猫の目のように変わる   *neko no me no yō ni kawaru*
"change like a cat's eye"
be in flux, change rapidly (in the twinkle of an eye); (of one's ideas or what says) be fickle, flip-flop, sing a different tune

---

○ 彼の言うことは猫の目のように変わるから、信じない方がいいよ。

Kare no iu koto wa neko no me no yō ni kawaru kara, shinjinai hō ga ii yo.

He's always changing what he says, so you'd better not believe him.

○ 原油価格が猫の目のように変わっている現在ではガソリンの末端価格設定も難しい。

Genyū-kakaku ga neko no me no yō ni kawatte iru genzai de wa gasorin no mattan kakaku-settei mo muzukashii.

Setting gasoline prices at the pumps is difficult at times like this when the price of crude is fluctuating.

○ ここ数年、東欧の政治情勢は猫の目のように変わっている。

Koko sūnen, tōō no seiji-jōsei wa neko no me no yō ni kawatte iru.

The political situation in Eastern Europe has been in flux over the past few years.

෴ From the quick reaction of a cat's pupil to small changes in light, this often unflattering expression can be used about change of all kinds but is most commonly used about a person's attitude, mood or opinion.

● 猫ばば（ババ）する   *nekobaba suru*   "cat poop"
pocket, find and keep

○ 目を離している間に、うちの猫に焼き魚を猫ばばされた。

Me o hanashite iru aida ni, uchi no neko ni yakizakana o neko-
   baba sareta.

When I wasn't looking, the cat made off with the fish I was broiling.

○ 次郎は母親の財布から1,000円猫ばばした。

Jiro wa haha-oya no saifu kara sen-en nekobaba shita.

Jiro filched (pocketed) ¥1,000 from his mother's wallet.

○ 彼女は拾った財布を猫ばばした。

Kanojo wa hirotta saifu o nekobaba shita.

She pocketed the wallet that she picked up on the street.

🐰 Always a verb, this often-heard expression comes from a cat's sanitary practice of covering its toilet with soil. The underlying notion here though is not one of cleaning up after oneself, but of hiding something and then acting innocent. It is most commonly used of something found and kept rather than returned, a wallet on the street or an umbrella in the train. *Baba* is baby talk for a bowel movement, something like "number two" or "pooh-pooh" in American English.

● 猫またぎ *nekomatagi* "cat straddling"
   a fish that tastes so bad even a cat would turn its nose up at it

○ なんだこの魚、猫またぎだなあ。

Nan da kono sakana, nekomatagi da nā.

What's this fish? No self-respecting cat would touch it!

○ こんな猫またぎよく食べれるなあ。

Konna nekomatagi yoku tabereru nā.

How can you eat this crap?

🐰 From the notion that even a fish-loving animal like a cat would step over and pass by a fish if it tasted bad enough. Not used about other foods.

● 猫もしゃくしも *neko mo shakushi mo* "cats and ladles too"
   everybody (and his brother), every mother's son, all the world, every Tom, Dick, and Harry; (of men) every swinging dick, every dog and his brother

○ 日本では冬になると、猫もしゃくしもスキーに出かける。

Nihon de wa fuyu ni naru to, neko mo shakushi mo sukī ni dekakeru.

Everybody and his brother hit the slopes in Japan during the winter.

○ ミニスカートが流行るのはいいけど、猫もしゃくしもとなるとどうもね。

Minisukāto ga hayaru no wa ii kedo, neko mo shakushi mo to naru to dōmo ne.

It's great when miniskirts are in style, but it's a bit much when everybody's gotta be wearing one.

🐰 *Shakushi* is another word for the more common *shamoji*, the wooden ladle used in Japanese homes to scoop rice from a rice cooker and into bowls. The expression comes from the fact that cats and ladles were common in all homes.

● 猫をかぶる　*neko o kaburu*　"put on the cat"

dissemble, feign (put on an act of) ignorance or innocence; be a wolf in sheep's clothing

---

○ 入学直後は猫をかぶっている学生が多い。

Nyūgaku-chokugo wa neko o kabutte iru gakusei ga ōi.

A lot of students watch their p's and q's (are on their best behavior) at the beginning of the academic year.

○ 真智子は叔父さんの家で一日中猫をかぶっていた。

Machiko wa ojisan no ie de, ichinichi-jū neko o kabbute ita.

Little Machiko put on her best behavior all day long at her uncle's house.

○ 無理を承知で頼むのだから、何を言われても猫をかぶって紳士でとおせ。

Muri o shōchi de tanomu no da kara, nani o iwarete mo neko o kabutte shinshi de tōse.

We're asking a lot of them, so no matter what they say to you just handle it as gentlemanly as you can.

🐰 The point here is that a person about whom this idiom is used is concealing his real personality and *acting* well behaved or demure. The noun form is *nekokaburi* 猫かぶり, meaning hypocrite, or a put-on.

ねずみ（鼠）　*nezumi* "rat, mouse"

☞　There is no linguistic distinction in Japanese between rats and mice—they are both just plain ol' *nezumi*. And they are numerous and common, facts that probably have given rise to many of the idioms that follow. While rats and mice have been held responsible for everything from ravaging granaries to spreading plague, it is important to note that at one time they were also believed to be the messengers of *Daikokuten,* a god of luck associated with wealth. This ambivalence toward rats and mice is manifest in the idioms that follow.

One interesting proverb featuring mice, *taizan-meidō shite nezumi ip-piki* 大（泰）山鳴動して鼠一匹, is used to describe a situation in which there was a lot of smoke but little fire, a terrible ruckus but little to show for it, as though the mountains had labored mightily only to bring forth a mouse.

The onomatopoeic cry of rats and mice is *chūchū* チュウチュウ. They are counted *ippiki* 一匹. When appearing as the first sign of the Chinese zodiac, *nezumi* is written 子.

● 頭の黒い鼠　*atama no kuroi nezumi*　"a black-headed rat"
　a snitcher, a thief in the family (who steals from the family)

○ 買い物から帰ってきたら引き出しの中の5千円札が無くなっていたので、これは頭の黒い鼠の仕業とピンときた。

Kaimono kara kaette kitara hikidashi no naka no gosen-en satsu ga nakunatte ita no de, kore wa atama no kuroi nezumi no shi-waza to pinto kita.

When I came home from shopping and discovered five thousand yen missing from the drawer, I knew it was the work of some-one in the family.

○ まさかわが家に頭の黒い鼠がいるとは思わなかった。

Masaka wagaya ni atama no kuroi nezumi ga iru to wa omowana-katta.

I never imagined we'd have a little snitcher in the family.

✌ Used all but exclusively of a person, often a child, either a family member or roommate, who pilfers from those living under the same roof. From the facts that rats prosper in and around human habitations, that things disappear when they forage successfully, and that, when some-thing in the home is discovered missing and a rat is unlikely to have an interest in that object, comes this idiom's attribution of blame to some-one in the household. The fact that Japanese have black hair provides the final element of the idiom, which is often used jocularly. Can be used in other group situations like co-workers in an office, when one discovers someone has been into the candy on one's desk.

● 窮鼠猫を嚙む　*kyūso neko o kamu*　"a cornered rat will bite a cat"
　a cornered rat can be dangerous; despair gives courage to a coward

---

○ 窮鼠猫を噛むと言うぐらいだから誘拐犯との交渉にはくれぐれも
　気をつけてくれ。

*Kyūso neko o kamu to iu gurai da kara yūkai-han to no kōshō ni
wa kuregure mo ki o tsukete kure.*

Remember that someone with his back to the wall will fight like
hell. So watch your ass when you go in to negotiate with the
kidnapper.

○ 包囲された反乱軍はまさに窮鼠猫を噛むの言葉どおり猛反撃を開
　始した。

*Hōi sareta hanran-gun wa masa ni kyūso neko o kamu no kotoba
dōri mō-hangeki o kaishi shita.*

With the desperation of a cornered rat, the surrounded rebels
launched a vicious counterattack.

⚘ Those of us who have been there know the strength lurking deep
within that allows even a weakling to stand up to someone of far superior
strength. That fabled superhuman strength, both psychological as well as
physical, that enables mothers to lift cars pinning their children is of a
different ilk, at least in Japanese. It is called *kajiba no bakajikara* 「火事
場の馬鹿力」, or "the amazing strength (one displays) at the scene of a
fire."

● こま鼠　*komanezumi*　"a top mouse"
　a hard (tireless) worker, a busy (eager) beaver, a busy bee

○ あの人は一日中こま鼠のようによく働く。

Ano hito wa ichinichi-jū komanezumi no yō ni yoku hataraku.

She works her tail off all day. / She keeps her nose to the grindstone all day.

○ こま鼠のように働いて、役に立たなくなったらクビなんてまっぴ
　ら御免だ。

*Komanezumi no yō ni hataraite, yaku ni tatanaku nattara kubi
nante mappira gomen da.*

No way I'm gonna spend my whole life with my nose to the grindstone only to be given my walking papers when I'm not needed
anymore.

⚘ The idiomatic use of this expression derives from the unusual behavior of the mutant *komanezumi* (top mouse) or *mainezumi* (dancing mouse).
Indigenous to Japan, the dancing mouse has a hereditary inner ear disorder resulting in an impaired sense of balance that causes it to chase its tail
in a frenzied whirlwind of senseless activity. Perhaps some wry observer
of the national work ethic found a parallel in this mouse's ceaseless spin-
ning round and round like a top (hence, its name) with the way people
work as though there were no more significant activity in life on the

archipelago. In usage, there is apparently no nuance of "senseless, repetitive activity." Found almost exclusively followed by *no yō ni hataraku*.

● どぶ鼠　*dobunezumi*　"a sewer rat"
a rat, a scoundrel

○ あの老舗が潰れたのはどぶ鼠のせいだ。
Ano shinise ga tsubureta no wa dobunezumi no sei da.
That long-established business went under thanks to the skulduggery of one of its employees.

○ このどぶ鼠が、ちょっと目を離すとろくなことしない。
Kono dobunezumi ga, chotto me o hanasu to roku na koto shinai.
You're always up to something the minute I take my eyes off you.

✌ Actually a brown, or Norway rat, this rodent is known for carrying the plague. Idiomatic usage is limited to an employee who embezzles from his employer or otherwise bites the hand that feeds him.

● ぬれ鼠　*nurenezumi*　"a wet rat"
(figuratively) a drowned rat, a person soaked to the bone

○ 彼は雨のふる街をあてもなく歩き回りぬれ鼠になった。
Kare wa ame no furu machi o ate mo naku arukimawari nurenezumi ni natta.
He got soaking (dripping) wet wandering around the city in the rain.

○ 全身ぬれ鼠で僕の部屋の前に立っていた彼女を見たときは一瞬お化けかと思ったよ。
Zenshin nurenezumi de boku no heya no mae ni tatte ita kanojo o mita toki wa isshun obake ka to omotta yo.
For a second I thought she was a ghost or something when I saw her standing outside my apartment soaked to the bone.

✌ Used to describe a person who looks pitiful and, of course, very wet, *nurenezumi* is used of a person who is fully clothed.

● ねずみ講　*nezumikō*　"a rat association"
a pyramid scheme

○ ねずみ講はマルチ商法と呼ばれ、日本では厳しく規制されている。
Nezumikō wa maruchi-shōhō to yobare, Nihon de wa kibishiku kisei sarete iru.

A kind of multilevel marketing plan, pyramid schemes are strictly regulated in Japan.

○ ねずみ講は姿を変え形を変え騙される消費者は後を絶たない。

Nezumikō wa sugata o kae katachi o kae damasareru shōhi-sha wa ato o tatanai.

The list of consumers taken in by pyramid schemes, which keep popping up in all shapes and forms, continues to grow.

☙ The idiom arises from the use in Japanese math classes of examples of rats having babies and the babies having babies ad infinitim to illustrate geometrical progression. See the next entry. One thing about these kinds of schemes in Japan, America, or anywhere else is that you can be sure to find a rat in the works somewhere.

● ねずみ算 *nezumizan* "count rats"
a pyramid, geometrical (exponential) increase

○ コンビニがねずみ算のようにあっという間に増えた。

Konbini ga nezumizan no yō ni atto iu ma ni fueta.

Convenience stores sprang up like mushrooms (multiplied like rabbits) overnight.

○ 彼女の借金はねずみ算式に増えていった。

Kanojo no shakkin wa nezumizan-shiki ni fuete itta.

Her debts were growing by leaps and bounds.

☙ As the second example indicates, the idiom commonly appears with the suffix *-shiki,* meaning way or fashion. Common verbs accompanying it include *fueru* and *zōka suru,* both of which mean increase. A possible translation for such usage might be "multiply like rabbits," although use would be limited to living things. The typical example given for teaching geometrical increase in "Japanese mathematics"—whatever that is—is that in January a pair of rats have twelve little ratlets. Rats being rats, a month later the twelve second-generation rats find an incestuous mate among themselves and together with the first generation rats have a bunch more little beady-eyed beasts. How many rats will there be in December? Well, there'll be a whole lot more than the neighborhood tabby can tolerate. Would you believe something like 2×7^{12} or about 27,600,000,000?

● ねずみ捕り *nezumitori* "a mousetrap"
a (police) speed trap, radar trap

○ こんなところでねずみ捕りなんかしやがって。

Konna tokoro de nezumitori nanka shiyagatte.

It pisses me off the way they put up speed traps in places like this.

○ この辺はよくねずみ捕りやっているから気をつけろよ。
Kono hen wa yoku nezumitori yatte iru kara ki o tsukero yo.
The cops love to set up radar traps around here, so watch out.

○ この間ねずみ捕りにやられて、反則金5万円払ったよ。
Kono aida nezumitori ni yararete, hansoku-kin goman-en haratta yo.
I got caught in a police speed trap the other day and paid a fine of ¥50,000.

✌ Slang. The Japanese police version of this universally denounced misuse of power, in keeping with many other Japanese practices, is employed when least likely to interrupt the conduct of business and most likely to infringe on the general population's right to enjoy what little free time they have; that is, on weekends and holidays, when the only people on the roads are out trying to relax and maybe go a little faster than the snail's pace that traffic and a national highway speed limit of 60 kph (36 mph) requires. The literal meaning, of which no examples are included here, is mousetrap.

● 鼠に引かれそう　*nezumi ni hikaresō*　"ready to be led away by a mouse"
(home alone and) feeling lonely; all by one's lonesome

○ 夜一人で残業してると、鼠に引かれそうになるわ。
Yoru hitori de zangyō shite 'ru to, nezumi ni hikaresō ni naru wa.
I really get lonely sometimes when I'm working late in the office all by myself.

○ えー、あなたが一人暮らし始めたの。夜、鼠に引かれないようにね。
Ē, anata ga hitorigurashi hajimeta no. Yoru, nezumi ni hikarenai yō ni ne.
Wow, you're living by yourself now! Don't let being alone at night get you down.

✌ We're talking real lonely here folks, so lonely that you'd let a rat come and take you away.

● 袋の（中の）ねずみ　*fukuro no (naka no) nezumi*　"a rat in a sack"
(of the person) *someone* trapped (like a rat); (of the situation) the jig is up

---

○ 君は袋のねずみだ、人質を解放して、投降しなさい。
Kimi wa fukuro no nezumi da, hitojichi o kaihō shite, tōkō shinasai.
You're trapped. Release your hostages and give yourself up.

○ あいつはもう袋のねずみ同然だ、どこへも逃げられない。
Aitsu wa mō fukuro no nezumi dōzen da, doko e mo nigerarenai.
The guy's up shit creek without a paddle. There's no place for him
to go.

○ 袋のねずみにされた容疑者は投降した。
Fukuro no nezumi ni sareta yōgi-sha wa tōkō shita.
Surrounded, the suspect gave himself up to the police

✌ From the plight of a rat that has been chased into a sack and has no
way to escape.

ひつじ （羊） *hitsuji* sheep

☞ This docile animal comes off about the same in Japan as its cousins
elsewhere, figuring in few idioms that would make it proud and several
that draw upon its perceived docility or stupidity. The word *hitsuji* is said
to have been formed from the *hi* for *hige* 髭, or beard, the *tsu* つ for the
possessive particle *no*, and the *ji* じ for cow. A sheep, in other words, is a
cow with a beard.

The sheep's bleat is *mēmē* メーメー. They are counted as *ippiki* 一匹 or
ittō 一頭. When the sheep is the eighth of the twelve signs in the Chinese
zodiac, it is written 未.

● 羊雲 *hitsujigumo* "a sheep cloud"
a fluffy (fleecy) cloud, a (altocumulus) floccus

○ 今日は絵に描いたような大きな羊雲が空に浮かんでいました。
*Kyō wa e ni kaita yō na ōki na hitsujigumo ga sora ni ukande
imashita.*
The sky was full of big, picture-perfect fleecy clouds today.

○ さとし君の描く雲はいつも羊雲だね。
Satoshi-kun no kaku kumo wa itsumo hitsujigumo da ne.
All the clouds you draw are big fluffy ones, Satoshi.

● 羊のよう （な／に） *hitsuji no yō (na/ni)* "like a sheep"
docile(ly), mousy (mousily), sheepish(ly), timerous(ly), very
quiet(ly)

○ 普段は羊のようにおとなしい彼が怒鳴ったんだからよっぽどひどいこと言われたに違いないよ。

Fudan wa hitsuji no yō ni otonashii kare ga donatta n' da kara yoppodo hidoi koto iwareta ni chigai nai yo.

For a sheepish (rabbity) guy like him to up and shout like that, somebody must have said something pretty bad to him.

○ 羊のような人ほど一度怒りだすと手が付けられないことが多いね。

Hitsuji no yō na hito hodo ichido okoridasu to te ga tsukerarenai koto ga ōi ne.

When someone who's usually a pussycat (milquetoast) explodes in anger, you've just got to keep your distance.

⚘ From the fact that sheep seldom rise up in rebellion against shepherds.

ひひ（狒狒）　*hihi*　baboon

☞ Since they are not native to Japan, it comes as no surprise that baboons figure in no parables or proverbs. That they are considered the closest thing in the wild kingdom to lecherous, middle-aged or elderly men is due, some suggest, to their resemblance to bearded old geezers. Baboons are counted *ittō* 一頭, and *hitori* 一人 (not really).

● ひひ　*hihi*　a baboon
a dirty old man, an old lech

○ このひひおやじ何を考えているんだ？

Kono hihi-oyaji nani o kangaete iru n' da?

You dirty old man, what've you got in mind now?

○ あのひひ爺酔ったふりして私のおっぱい触りまくったのよ。

Ano hihi-jijī yotta furi shite watashi no oppai sawarimakutta no yo.

That old lech acted like he was drunk so he could feel me up.

⚘ Commonly followed by *jijī* 爺 or *oyaji* おやじ.

ぶた（豚）　*buta*　pig, swine

☞ In the absence of the Vietnamese strain of potbellied ambassadors of warmth and refinement, the three hundred or so varieties of swine known to Japan remain reviled as filthy, ugly beasts, a reputation these descendants of wild boars have been encumbered with, perhaps due to the conditions of their domesticity, i.e., living in sties. Although cops don't get called *buta* by protestors, jails do earn the unofficial appellation *butabako*, or pig box, presumably for the unsanitary conditions encountered inside. The pig's oink is *būbū* ブーブー(the same as a fart), and it is counted *ippiki* 一匹 or *ittō* 一頭.

● 豚　*buta*　a pig

1. (someone ugly) a pig, two-bagger; (dirty or slovenly) a pig, slob, scuzzball; (someone who is fat or overeats) a pig, a chow hound; (someone stupid) a dumbell, fool, dimwit, knucklehead, airhead

---

○ この豚！
Kono buta!
You swine (pig, fat ass, dimwit)!

○ あの豚野郎、今度会ったらただじゃおかねえ。
Ano butayarō, kondo attara tada ja okanē.
That mother! He's gonna get what's coming to him next time.

& Used to revile someone, it is often followed by *yarō* 野郎, when describing a man, and *onnamata* 女叉 when referring to a woman who is an object of scorn.

---

2. (of such things as a bad or losing hand in cards or a losing lottery ticket) a loser; nothing; come up short

---

○ またブタだ！
Mata buta da!
Not another shitty hand!

○ この間宝くじ2万円も買ったのに全部ブタだったよ。
Kono aida takarakuji niman-en mo katta no ni zenbu buta datta yo.
I shelled out 20,000 yen for lottery tickets a while ago, and damned if every last one of them wasn't a loser.

● 豚小屋　*butagoya*　"a pigpen"
(a small, filthy house, apartment, or room) a pigpen, pigsty

○ なんだこの部屋はまるで豚小屋だなあ、すこしは掃除しろよ。
Nan da kono heya wa maru de butagoya da nā, sukoshi wa sōji shiro yo.
God, what a pigsty! Ever thought about cleaning it up a little?

○ こんな豚小屋から早く引っ越したいよ。
Konna butagoya kara hayaku hikkoshitai yo.

I can't wait to move out of this dump.

✌ From the mistaken belief that pigs are filthy animals, although anyone who's ever let a bunch of them in the house knows they always wipe their hooves at the door.

● 豚に真珠　*buta ni shinju*　"pearls to pigs"
casting pearls before swine; a waste

---

o そんな高級なピアノ買ったって、豚に真珠だよ。
Sonna kōkyū na piano katta tte, buta ni shinju da yo.
Buying an expensive piano like that for him is like casting pearls before swine.

o こんな年寄りがワープロ持っても、豚に真珠ですよ。
Konna toshiyori ga wāpuro motte mo, buta ni shinju desu yo.
What a waste it is for an old guy like me to have a word processor.

✌ A linguistic import, this comes from the New Testament. Although there is no consensus, some feel this expression is used exclusively about material objects rather than abstractions.

☞ *neko ni koban* 猫に小判

● 豚箱　*butabako*　"pig box"
a jail, the clink, the cooler, the slammer

---

o 俺、若い頃極道して豚箱入れられたことあるんだ。
Ore, wakai koro gokudō shite butabako irerareta koto aru n' da.
I went astray when I was young and ended up doing hard time.

o お前そんなことしてると豚箱にぶち込まれるぞ。
Omae sonna koto shite 'ru to butabako ni buchikomareru zo.
Keep it up and you'll be cooling your heels in jail.

✌ From the filth, crowded conditions (previously?) encountered in such places.

● 豚もおだてりゃ木に登る　*buta mo odaterya ki ni noboru*
"even a pig will climb a tree if you flatter it"
flattery will get you a long way

---

o 「えー、あの人がその借金の面倒みるって本当に約束したの。」
"Ē, ano hito ga sono shakkin no mendō miru tte hontō ni yakusoku shita no."

"No way! He really promised he'd loan you the money?"

「豚もおだてりゃ木に登るっていうだろう。」

"Buta mo odaterya ki ni noboru tte iu darō."

"Like they say, a little flattery goes a long way."

○ 豚もおだてりゃ木に登るっていうけど、どうやってあの女優に出演を承諾させたの？

Buta mo odaterya ki ni noboru tte iu kedo, dō yatte ano joyū ni shutsuen o shōdaku saseta no?

I know a little flattery will go a long way, but just how did you talk that actress into agreeing to appear in the production?

むじな（狢）　*mujina*　badger

☞　Also called a hole bear, or *anaguma* 穴熊, and often confused with the raccoon dog, or *tanuki* 狸, the badger shares an image of persistence with its Western counterpart, although such has not found its way into idiomatic usage. Still, this member of the weasel family comes off little better in Japanese than in English, figuring in a single idiom, and that with negative connotations. Badgers are counted *ippiki* 一匹.

● 同じ穴のむじな　*onaji ana no mujina*　"badgers from the same den"

birds of a feather, (be) just like (no different/no better than) the others

---

○ 今だからお前善人面しているが、元はヤクザ俺とは同じ穴のむじなだ。

Ima da kara omae zennin-zura shite iru ga, moto wa yakuza ore to wa onaji ana no mujina da.

You can play Mr. Nice Guy now, but you've got a past just like I do.

○ 今の日本はどこの政党が政権をとっても変わりなし、政治家は皆同じ穴のむじな。

Ima no Nihon wa doko no seitō ga seiken o totte mo kawari nashi, seiji-ka wa mina onaji ana no mujina.

It doesn't make a bit of difference which party is in power in Japan today, politicians are all the same, you can't tell one from another.

モグラ *mogura* mole

☞ Bigger than earthworms maybe, but no worthier of being hailed as earth dragons (土竜, which is one kanji-fication of their name), these little mammals have finally burrowed their way into the language in the form of at least one fairly recent, but widely heard, idiom that you'll have to dig to find in Japanese dictionaries. But more about that later. First, the name *mogura* has a history as intricate as any tunnel a mole might dig. It derives, according to one source, from the verb *uguromotsu*, which means to mound dirt, something readers who know anything about ancient Japan will recognize as an activity that bordered on becoming a national obsession for three or four centuries some fifteen hundred years ago, at least for the rich and famous. Anyway, for those who are still with us, there's a noun, *uguromochi*—presumably having something to do with the mounding of dirt and, not surprisingly, another name for a mole—that underwent a transformation to become *muguromochi*, and was shaken up again and abbreviated to give us the word we all can now appropriately appreciate, *mogura*. Now if you think this is making a mountain out of a molehill, well, you're right. But you'll have to find another way to say that in Japanese, because that's one idiom that doesn't come out the same. Moles are counted *ippiki* 一匹.

● もぐらたたき *mogura-tataki* "mole pounding"
an endless battle

○ 週末の暴走族取締まりはもぐらたたきと同じだ。

Shūmatsu no bōsōzoku-torishimari wa mogura-tataki to onaji da.

Trying to round up motorcycle gangs on the weekends is an endless battle.

○ 電話ボックスに張り付けてあるカードに、警察は摘発に乗り出しているが、まるでもぐらたたき状態である。

Denwa-bokkusu ni haritsukete aru kādo ni, keisatsu wa tekihatsu ni noridashite iru ga, maru de moguratataki-jōtai de aru.

The police are trying to do something about the stickers that are pasted all over phone booths, but the minute one place is cleared out they go up someplace else.

🐾 From the popular game found in many arcades in Japan. Put your money in, stand in front of a waist-high platform full of holes, and wait for the moles (*mogura*) to start popping their heads up. The idea is to whack (*tataku*) as many of them as you can in the allotted time with a large plastic mallet. Great fun for the intellectually challenged. By extension, the idiom is used to describe attempts to eradicate crime or antisocial behavior, like having a good time, only to find that the behavior resurfaces somewhere else soon thereafter.

☜ *itachigokko* いたちごっこ

ろば（驢馬）　*roba* donkey

☞ As rare as this hard-working little beast is in the land, it is even rarer in the language. Its fabled stubbornness is not enough to warrant its inclusion in any idioms, but those ears seem to have done the trick. In fact, a second name for the donkey in Japanese derives from its oversized audio equipment, *usagiuma* 兎馬, or literally rabbit horse. Whatever they are called, they are counted *ippiki* 一匹 or *ittō* 一頭.

● ろばの耳　*roba no mimi* "donkey ears"
　(be) all ears

○ 先生達がひそひそ話してたから、思わずろばの耳になった。

Sensei-tachi ga hisohiso hanashite 'ta kara, omowazu roba no mimi ni natta.

I couldn't help pricking up my ears to hear what the teachers were whispering about.

○ 電車の中で私のこと噂している高校のときの友達がいて、ろばの耳になっちゃったよ。

Densha no naka de watashi no koto uwasa shite iru kōkō no toki no tomodachi ga ite, roba no mimi ni natchatta yo.

I was all ears when some of my friends from high school were talking about me in the train.

✤ Used jocularly of people trying so hard to hear something that they could benefit from larger ears than the gods gave them. Appears most commonly followed by *ni naru*.

2

爬虫類と両生類
REPTILES & AMPHIBIANS

No, we're not talking about those crusty antediluvians who always seem to vote and seldom miss a chance to exercise their right to the silver seats; you can call them a lot of different things in Japan, but reptile is not among them.

Although recent trends in pet ownership—snakes and lizards are in—*may* indicate a sea change in Japanese attitudes toward reptiles and amphibians, it is more likely that there will just be an increase in scaly roadkill on the nation's highways and byways as fickle owners, tiring of stepping on their trendy friends, turn them loose in the concrete jungle to join the growing numbers of parrots and other discarded companions. Meanwhile, the first thing that still comes to most Japanese minds at the mention of creepy-crawly things is dislike and disgust.

蛙 *kaeru* or *kawazu* frog

☞ If you're French you can relax; no Japanese is going to call you a *kaeru* because of your nation's nuclear policies. They might call you something else, but at least it won't be "Frog." These most common of amphibians have yet to be driven into extinction in Japan, less, no doubt, because of environmental concern than longstanding governmental protection of rice farmers, rice paddies, and hence our vocal green buddies, who enjoy a worldwide reputation for forewarning of rain by croaking. It is from their croaking, which, by the onomatopoeic way, is *kerokero* ケロ ケロ or *kuwa'-kuwa'* クワックワッ, that Japanese children, especially those brought up in the country and have heard the soothing evening serenade, often head for home on a warm summer evening after a day of play intoning their own homophonic play on words, *Kaeru ga naku kara kaero* 蛙がなくから帰ろ, literally "The frogs are croaking so let's go home."

The *kerokero* voice of a frog is said to resemble the Japanese phrase *kaerō*, or "Let's go home." The infinitive of the verb "to return" or "to go home" *kaeru* is also a homophone for the word for frog. Some simple words and phrases of interest include *kaeruashi* 蛙足, literally "frogleg," and meaning the frog kick as employed in the breast stroke, which in turn, and perhaps not coincidentally, is called *kaeru-oyogi* 蛙足泳ぎ, or frog swim. There is also *kaerutobi* 蛙跳び, or leapfrog, though only in the sense of a game children play; and *kaeru-nyōbō* 蛙女房, a complicated play on words that originates from the fact that a frog's eyes are on the top of its head (目が上にある, *me ga ue ni aru*) and that a common word for wife in Japanese, *tsuma* 妻, can also be pronounced *me,* and if she is older, she is above, or *ue,* her husband; hence a *kaeru-nyōbō* is a woman who is older than her husband.

Frogs are counted *ippiki* 一匹.

● 井の中の蛙 *i no naka no kawazu* "a frog in a well"
a babe in the woods, a naive person

○ 井の中の蛙になるのを恐れて彼女は独立を決心した。

I no naka no kawazu ni naru no o osorete kanojo wa dokuritsu o kesshin shita.

Afraid that she would end up not knowing anything about the ways of the world, she resolved to set out on her own.

○ たかが地区大会に優勝したぐらいで有頂天になっては井の中の蛙じゃないか。

Takaga chiku-taikai ni yūshō shita gurai de uchōten ni natte wa i no naka no kawazu ja nai ka.

Don't you think getting all worked up over something like winning at the regional level is a bit parochial?

⚓ Shortened from the now less common proverb, *I no naka no kawazu taikai o shirazu* 井の中の蛙大海を知らず, or "The frog in the well knows nothing of the great ocean."

● 蛙の子は蛙 *kaeru no ko wa kaeru* "the child of a frog is a frog"
1. like father, like son; like mother, like daughter; what is born of a cat will catch mice

---

○ 蛙の子は蛙、手先が器用なのは親譲りだ。

Kaeru no ko wa kaeru, tesaki ga kiyō na no wa oyayuzuri da.
I get my manual dexterity from my parents. It's in the blood.

○ やっぱり蛙の子は蛙だね、彼の息子も結局会社を辞めて家業を継いだよ。

Yappari kaeru no ko wa kaeru da ne, kare no musuko mo kekkyoku kaisha o yamete kagyō o tsuida yo.

His son's a chip off the old block, all right. In the end, he quit his job and followed in his father's footsteps, taking over the family business.

2. ordinary parents have ordinary children

○ 俺の子供が東大なんて入れるものじゃないよ、蛙の子は蛙、変な夢を見たと思って諦めよう。

Ore no kodomo ga Tōdai nante haireru mono ja nai yo. Kaeru no ko wa kaeru, hen na yume o mita to omotte akirameyō.

I guess it was too much to expect that one of my kids could get into the University of Tokyo. Better just chalk it up to experience, I guess.

➠ *tobi ga taka o umu* 鳶が鷹を生む

● おたまじゃくし *otamajakushi* "tadpole"
1. a musical note; music

○ 俺おたまじゃくしに弱いんだよね。
Ore otamajakushi ni yowai n' da yo ne.
I wish I could read music.

🐰 From a pollywog's chimerical resemblance to a musical note.

2. a ladle

○ ちょっとそこのおたまじゃくし取って。
Chotto soko no otamajakushi totte.
Get that ladle for me, would you?

🐰 From the physical resemblance of the shape of a ladle to that of a pollywog.

● 蛙の面に小便 *kaeru no tsura ni shonben (shōben)* "piss on a frog's face"
(like) water off a duck's back, not faze *someone*

○ 先生がもう卒業出来ないって言っても、あいつには蛙の面に小便 だよ。

Sensei ga mō sotsugyō dekinai tte itte mo, aitsu ni wa kaeru no tsura ni shonben da yo.

It doesn't faze him if teachers tell him that he's not going to graduate; he could care less.

○ 皆がいくらいじめてもまるで蛙の面に小便、あいつは鈍いのか強 いのかわかんないね。

Mina ga ikura ijimete mo maru de kaeru no tsura ni shonben, aitsu wa nibui no ka tsuyoi no ka wakannai ne.

No matter how bad a time everybody gives him, it's like water off a duck's back. It's hard to tell if he's really tough or just a bit dim.

⚥ A graphic if disgusting idiom illustrating the futility of talking to a person who is either too brazen, dull-witted, or insensitive to listen. Less common is *kaeru no tsura ni mizu,* or "water on a frog's face."

● がま口　*gamaguchi*　"a toad's mouth"
1. a (coin) purse

○ 今どき、がま口なんていう人はあまりいないよ。
Imadoki, gamaguchi nante iu hito wa amari inai yo.
Nobody calls a coin purse a *gamaguchi* anymore.

---

2. (literally) a big mouth

○ あの漫画の主人公の特徴はがま口のような口です。
Ano manga no shujinkō no tokuchō wa gamaguchi no yō na kuchi desu.
The hero of that cartoon's got a giant mouth.

⚥ *Gama* is shortened from *gamagaeru,* or bullfrog. Frogs are also sometimes called *gama.*

┌───┐
│ すっぽん　*suppon*　"soft-shelled turtle" │
└───┘

☞ In Japan the lowly mud turtle figures in a few expressions that will give you a pretty clear idea of the esteem in which this freshwater terrapin is held. *Suppon* is also slang for "dick," as in "purple turkey neck," "one-eyed trouser mouse," or any of the hundreds of English words for the penis, from a some physical resemblance between the male member and the turtle's head and neck. Coming off better in questions of the palate, its meat, the soft-shelled turtle's that is, is prized for use in por-

ridge, especially during the winter months.
Soft-shelled turtles are counted *ippiki* 一匹.

● すっぽん　*suppon*　"a soft-shelled turtle"
a persistent person, bulldog, badger

○ あの刑事は俗に「すっぽん」と呼ばれている。
Ano keiji wa zoku ni "suppon" to yabarete iru.
That dick is known on the street as the bulldog.

○ 芸能レポーターはすっぽんのようにその俳優を追い回した。
Geinō-repōtā wa suppon no yō ni sono haiyū o oimawashita.
Reporters on the celebrity beat were badgering that actor every-
place he went.

※ From the observation that soft-shelled turtles have strong jaws, and
once they glom onto prey or fingers they never let go.

● 月とすっぽん　*tsuki to suppon*　"the moon and a soft-
shelled turtle"
as different as night and day (chalk from cheese), a whale
of a difference

○ 一番弟子といってもやっぱり先生と比べたら月とすっぽんだよ。
*Ichiban-deshi to itte mo yappari sensei to kurabetara tsuki to sup-
pon da yo.*
She may be the professor's protégé, but there's a world of difference between them.

○ さすがここのケーキおいしいわ、あの新宿のケーキと比べたら月
とすっぽんね。
*Sasuga koko no kēki oishii wa, ano Shinjuku no kēki to kurabetara
tsuki to suppon ne.*
The pastries here are truly sublime, so much better than those we
had in Shinjuku the other day.

※ From the observation that although the round shape of a soft-shelled
turtle's carapace may resemble the moon, the two are vastly different
(and the latter much more esteemed for its beauty).

とかげ（蜥蜴）　*tokage*　lizard

☞　Like other reptiles, the lizard doesn't have much of a following—
there are no Lizard Days in Japan. There was a bit of excitement in the

late 1980s when Japanese TV viewers were introduced to the frilled lizard by Japan's ad industry in a Mitsubishi Motors commercial for its Mirage model. But that has all died down at the time of this writing, and the little scamps are probably running around happily in the natural light of the Australian desert again (at least those that survived the rigors of commercial filmmaking).

Lizards are counted *ippiki* 一匹.

● とかげのしっぽ切り *tokage no shippo-kiri* "breaking off a lizard's tail"

pass the buck to one's subordinate; save one's ass by sacrificing an underling, throw someone to the lions (wolves)

○ 市役所の汚職事件の処罰はとかげのしっぽ切りで終わってしまった。
Shi-yakusho no oshoku-jiken no shobatsu wa tokage no shippo-kiri de owatte shimatta.
The corruption scandal at city hall ended with subordinates taking the rap (being the fall guys/patsies) for the bigwigs.

○ オウム真理教のら致事件はとかげのしっぽ切りで終わらないだろう。
Ōmu Shinri-kyō no rachi-jiken wa tokage no shippo-kiri de owaranai darō.
The Supreme Truth Sect abductions won't end with the underlings being thrown to the lions (going to the gallows for the real criminals).

𝔐 From a lizard's ability to detach its tail and regenerate another when pursued by children or other less rapacious predators .

蛇 *hebi* snake, serpent

☞ Less in the grass than the paddies, snakes nevertheless fare little better in Japanese than English, their lowly position inspiring the linguistic muse to a few waggish observations about them not needing feet, or humans inviting trouble by rustling around in the bushes where snakes repose. In need of some serious PR work in Japan, snakes are commonly held to be mysterious, fearsome, loathsome, and creepy. Snakes were formerly thought to enjoy eternal life because of their ability to molt.

Snakes are fairly common in Japan but seldom poisonous. Only the *mamushi*, a kind of pit viper, is widely distributed and feared (for good reason). One snake, the boa, or *uwabami* 蟒蛇, has lent its moniker to a person who drinks a lot, perhaps from a folk tale in which an eight-headed, eight-tailed snake is conquered and a beautiful maiden rescued by a prince who gets the beast drunk by bringing eight casks from which it quaffs its fill. One less common proverb not included as an entry, *ja no michi wa hebi* 蛇の道は蛇, literally "a snake (knows) the path of snakes," is similar to our English "Set a thief to catch a thief" or, more commonly among children, "It takes one to know one."

When written as the sixth sign of the Chinese and Japanese zodiac or calendar, the character 巳 is employed. Snakes are counted *ippiki* 一匹 or, less commonly, *ichio* 一尾.

● 蛇足　*dasoku*　"snake's feet"
unnecessary, extraneous; tits on a boar

○ そんな話は蛇足だ。
Sonna hanashi wa dasoku da.
That's completely unnecessary.

○ 彼女がその講演で最後に話したことは蛇足だった。
Kanojo ga sono kōen de saigo ni hanashita koto wa dasoku datta.
What she said at the very end of the lecture amounted more and less to flogging a dead horse.

○ 蛇足ですが、私は昆虫採集が趣味です。
Dasoku desu ga, watashi wa konchū-saishū ga shumi desu.
Needless to say, collecting insects is my hobby.

○ このレポートは蛇足の部分が多すぎる。
Kono repōto wa dasoku no bubun ga ōsugiru.
There's too much padding in this paper. / This report has got a lot of fluff in it.

🐍 Can be used both of objects and of behavior. From an ancient Chinese tale of some friends who bet a round of drinks on who among them could paint a snake the fastest. One of the men was much quicker at the task than his friends and decided in his leisure to add legs to his creation. Upon seeing this, another painter asked how he could put legs on a reptile that originally had none, and he relieved the man of his prize before he could quaff his victory libation.

● 長蛇の列　*chōda no retsu*　"a long snake line"
a long line (queue)

○ そのラーメン屋の前は昼どきになると長蛇の列ができる。
Sono rāmen-ya no mae wa hirudoki ni naru to chōda no retsu ga dekiru.
There's always a long line of people in front of that ramen shop when lunchtime rolls around.

○ 祭日のディズニーランドはどこのアトラクションも長蛇の列だ。

Saijitsu no Dizunīrando wa doko no atorakushon mo chōda no retsu da.

There's a long line snaking around in front of every attraction at Disneyland on holidays.

🐍 From the resemblance of a line of people to the body of a snake.

● 蛇ににらまれた（見込まれた）蛙　*hebi in niramareta (mikomareta) kaeru* "a frog being watched by a snake" cannot move or get away, be frozen in fear, transfixed (paralyzed) with fear; (like) a deer caught in the headlights

---

○ 浮気の現場を妻におさえられて彼はまるで蛇ににらまれた蛙だった。

Uwaki no genba o tsuma ni osaerarete kare wa maru de hebi ni niramareta kaeru datta.

He was frozen with fear when his wife caught him in bed with another woman.

○ 蛇に見込まれた蛙のように彼女はその男の言うなりだった。

Hebi ni mikomareta kaeru no yō ni kanojo wa sono otoko no iu nari datta.

Like a deer caught in a car's oncoming headlights, she found herself at his beck and call.

🐍 Graphic metaphorical expression illustrating the paralysis induced by fear when prey are confronted by a natural enemy.

● 蛇の生殺し　*hebi no namagoroshi* "half-killing a snake"
1. (literally) leave something half-dead (on its last legs)

○ その部隊は村民全員を蛇の生殺し状態にして、村を去った。

Sono butai wa sonmin zen'in o hebi no namagoroshi jōtai ni shite, mura o satta.

The unit left the villagers to die after beating them to within an inch of their life.

○ マスコミがこぞって犯人扱いにしたので、まるで蛇の生殺し状態となったそのタレントはとうとう自殺に追い込まれた。

Masukomi ga kozotte hannin-atsukai ni shita no de, maru de hebi no namagoroshi jōtai to natta sono tarento wa tōtō jisatsu ni oikomareta.

Branded as a criminal by the press and left twisting in the wind, the celebrity was driven to commit suicide.

🐇 From the notion of beating a snake half dead (within an inch of its life) and then leaving it to die; the kind of thing young boys seem compelled to do.

---

2. leave something half-done (finished), do something half-assed

○ あの人の仕事はいつでも蛇の生殺しだね。

Ano hito no shigoto wa itsu de mo hebi no namagoroshi da ne.

Every job he does is either half-finished or half-baked.

○ うちのような零細企業がこの不景気に銀行の融資を打ち切られたら蛇の生殺しだ。

Uchi no yō na reisai-kigyō ga kono fu-keiki ni ginkō no yūshi o uchikiraretara hebi no namagoroshi da.

Small businesses like ours will be left high and dry if banks cut us off in the middle of an economic downturn like this.

● やぶ蛇　*yabuhebi*　"a snake in the brush"
ask for it (trouble), stir up a hornets' nest; wake a sleeping dog, not know when to leave well enough alone, put *one's* foot in it

---

○ やぶ蛇になるからそのことは話さない方がいいよ。

Yabuhebi ni naru kara sono koto wa hanasanai hō ga ii yo.

You probably shouldn't mention it, or you'll just stir up a hornets' nest. / You'll just be asking for trouble if you bring that up.

○ お父さんに小遣いせびったら、やぶ蛇になっちゃって、成績のことで怒られちゃった。

Otōsan ni kozukai sebittara, yabuhebi ni natchatte, seiseki no koto de okorarechatta.

I was buggin' my old man for some spending money when the shit hit the fan, and he started in on me about my grades.

○ この件では仕入れ先にクレームをつけない方がいいよ。支払いのことを問題にされたらやぶ蛇になる。

Kono ken de wa shiire-saki ni kurēmu o tsukenai hō ga ii yo. Shiharai no koto o mondai ni saretara yabuhebi ni naru.

In this case, we'd better not register a complaint against the supplier. If they bring up the matter of payment, we'll find ourselves with a different can of worms.

🐇 Shortened from *yabu o tsutsuite hebi o dasu* 藪をつついて蛇を出す, or literally, "poke around in the brush and drive out a snake," it means to say or do something uncalled for and thereby worsen one's position.

● 竜頭蛇尾　*ryūtōdabi*　"head of a dragon, tail of a snake"
get off to a good start but end up fizzling (petering) out; start with a bang and end with a whimper

---

○ 都市計画はバブル崩壊で竜頭蛇尾に終わる恐れが出てきた。
Toshi-keikaku wa baburu hōkai de ryūtō-dabi ni owaru osore ga dete kita.
There's a good possibility that the urban renewal plan will peter out now that the economic bubble has burst.

○ 政府の所得倍増計画は竜頭蛇尾に終わった。
Seifu no shotoku-baizō-keikaku wa ryūtōdabi ni owatta.
The government's plans for doubling income started with a fanfare but ended in a fizzle.

※ This colorful expression stems from the observation that things that start off with a bang seldom end with such great fanfare. The expression is most commonly accompanied by the verb *owaru* 終わる.

3

鳥類
BIRDS

Japan is home to more than five hundred species of birds including natives, denizens, and seasonal visitors. The expressions collected below have their various origins in fables, folk tales, and observations of avian characteristics and behavior, and draw upon a native wisdom and humor that likens a short, heavyset person's bustling waddle to a goose hurrying to check out a fire (*ahiru no kaji mimai* あひるの火事 見舞い), or sees in the hard-working but underappreciated employee a duck that appears to swim effortlessly over the water but is actually paddling madly beneath the surface (*kamo no mizu kaki* 鴨の水掻き).

As in English, the bird's lofty position gives it a better view of things and the Japanese word for such a "bird's-eye" view is *chōkan* 鳥瞰.

う （鵜）　*u* cormorant

☞ Fables in the *Nihon Shoki* and the *Kojiki* depict the thatching of special maternity huts with cormorant feathers. They describe women in labor within these huts as holding a cormorant feather in the belief that doing so would guarantee a safe birth, probably from the observation that the bird is capable of disgorging intact fish it has swallowed whole. Another folk belief held that intoning *u no nodo* 鵜の喉 or *u no tori* 鵜の鳥 would dislodge a fish bone caught in one's throat. The cormorant is still used to fish in Japan, with a rope tied around its neck to prevent it from swallowing before it has been forced to disgorge the fish it has captured. Thought in the West to be gluttonous, and lending its name to a person so viewed, this cousin of the pelican has no such reputation in Japan.

Cormorants are counted *ichiwa* 一羽.

● 鵜呑み *u-nomi* "swallow (whole) like a cormorant"
swallow (something) whole; swallow a story hook, line, and sinker; be gullible

---

○ 何でもかんでも鵜呑みはよくない。
Nandemo-kandemo u-nomi wa yoku nai.
You can't go around believing everything you hear. / Don't be so gullible.

○ 鵜呑みは禁物だ、この件に関してはほかの人の意見も参考にしよう。
U-nomi wa kinmotsu da, kono ken ni kanshite wa hoka no hito no iken mo sankō ni shiyō.
Can't take things at face value. Better get another opinion of what's coming down here.

○ 彼のいうことを鵜呑みにするのは危険だ。
Kare no iu koto o u-nomi ni suru no wa kiken da.
You're just asking for trouble if you take him at his word. / You've got to take what he says with a grain of salt or you'll be sorry.

○ あなたのいうことをそのまま鵜呑みにするわけにはいかない。
Anata no iu koto o sono mama u-nomi ni suru wake ni wa ikanai.
You can't really expect me to take your word for it.

✌ From the way a cormorant swallows fish whole to be digested in its stomach.

● 鵜の目鷹の目 *u no me taka no me* "a cormorant's eye, a hawk's eye"
scrutinize, pour over, look over carefully; keep *one's* eyes peeled (for)

○ 私の姑は鵜の目鷹の目で私のあらを探している。
Watashi no shūtome wa u no me taka no me de watashi no ara o sagashite iru.
My mother-in-law's always on the lookout for any little fault she can find in me.

○ 会社が倒産しそうなので、鵜の目鷹の目で彼は転職先を探している。
Kaisha ga tōsan shisō na no de, u no me taka no me de kare wa tenshoku-saki o sagashite iru.
He is keeping his eyes peeled for a new job because the company he's with now is on the ropes.

✌ From the fact that both the cormorant and the hawk are sharp-eyed.

うぐいす（鶯）　*uguisu*　bush warbler

☞　Intimately associated with the early-blooming plum in traditional poetry and painting, the arrival of this melodious harbinger of spring to the garden remains an annual event commented upon to neighbors and friends by many suburban Japanese. So closely is this songster linked with the plum, that the two are sometimes paired together in the metaphoric description of a perfect match. Although keeping the bird caged to enjoy its song now requires legal authorization, the practice was once common, with competitions called *uguisu-awase* , literally "the bringing together of bush warblers," held to judge the most beautiful warble. (The bird's song is so highly esteemed that the word *uguisu* has become a metaphor for a woman with a beautiful voice.) So-called nightingale floors—only a slight misnomer—have even been designed to squeak—er, that is, sing—like the warbler and, the explanation goes, forewarn wary military leaders of the late-night approach of assassins. In one practice, thankfully no longer common, the warbler's excrement was mixed with rice bran and used as a scrub for the skin.

The bush warbler's song is *hōhokekyo* ホーホケキョ. It is counted *ip-piki* 一匹 or *ichiwa* 一羽.

● うぐいす嬢　*uguisujō*　"a young woman warbler"
a woman, usually young, who sings or speaks with a beauti-ful voice; woman announcer over a PA system

---

○ 彼女の声はうぐいす嬢にピッタリだ。

Kanojo no koe wa uguisu-jō ni pittari da.

Her voice is perfect (just right) for a PA announcer.

○ 選挙の時のうぐいす嬢はいいアルバイトになるそうだ。

Senkyo no toki no uguisu-jō wa ii arubaito ni naru sō da.

They say that elections are a great time for young female PA an-nouncers to get well-paying part-time jobs.

○ うぐいす嬢の声は、バッターボックスに立ったイチローへの歓声にかき消された。

Uguisujō no koe wa, battā bokkusu ni tatta Ichirō e no kansei ni kakikesareta.

When Ichirō stood in the batter's box, the female announcer's voice was drowned out by the cheering.

✌ Use of this expression seems to be limited to women announcing sporting events in a stadium, standing in the front of buses explaining inane facts about bad architecture and obscure personages, or riding around in sound cars bristling with loudspeakers mindlessly waving their white-gloved hands at anyone who happens to look up, and repeating a few rote expressions that have absolutely nothing to do with the political candidate for whose campaign they have been optimistically hired to lend an air of freshness—an all but impossible task in contemporary Japan.

● 鶯鳴かせたこともある　*uguisu nakaseta koto mo aru*　"has even made the bush warbler sing"
used to be quite a looker, used to have men wrapped around her little finger

---

○ うちのおばあちゃん鶯鳴かせたこともあるほど可愛かったらしいわよ。
Uchi no obāchan uguisu nakaseta koto mo aru hodo kawaikatta rashii wa yo.
My grandmother used to have to beat men off with a stick, she was so good-looking.

○ そこの角のタバコ屋のおばさん、若いときはちょっとしたもので鶯鳴かせたこともあるらしいわよ。
Soko no kado no tabakoya no obasan, wakai toki wa chotto shita mono de uguisu nakaseta koto mo aru rashii wa yo.
From what I hear, the woman who runs that cigarette shop on the corner used to be quite the talk of the town.

☺ In a male/female role reversal, this idiom equates a woman with a plum tree and a man with a warbler so attracted to the tree's beautiful blossoms that it breaks out in song. The thinking here is from the observation that warblers are often seen singing among the spring blossoms of the plum, and that even a wizened old plum tree was once young and had beautiful blossoms that attracted bush warblers; hence, while a woman may no longer be young and beautiful, she once had her pick of men.

おうむ（鸚鵡）*ōmu* parrot

☞　Although this import's ability to mimic sounds, particularly the human voice, is its only quality worthy of linguistic mention, the sky above Japanese urban parks (as exaggerated reports would have it) is darkened by flocks of parrots that have escaped the wire and wicker confines of their cramped cages and banded together in the few remaining natural areas in the cities to live in freedom, eking out a subsistence among the concrete edifices that loom above them. Yeah, well. While it may be true that parrots occasionally escape from their cages—sightings of small flocks have been documented in Tokyo's parks—the "problem" is undoubtedly overstated. Having said that, it must be remarked that psittacosis, or parrot fever, a disease that can infect humans, is fairly common among the nation's imported birds, and as early as ten years ago it had spread to nearly half the dogs and 10 percent of the cats brought into Tokyo's pet shelters. It sounds like the makings of a B movie, *Revenge of the Parrots*.

At this writing, the first thing that comes to mind for most Japanese upon hearing the word *ōmu* is the discredited religious sect of Shoko Asahara, whose Aum Shinrikyo appears ("appears" added by my timorous editor!) to have been behind the poison gas attacks in Tokyo's subways in early 1995 as well as numerous other murders, extortions, and, on a lighter note, one of the most entertaining political campaigns in recent memory, during which dozens of followers donned papier-mâché heads modeled after Asahara's dour phiz and "parroted" ridiculous ditties. But this *ōmu* is not of the natural world, deriving instead from the two phonemes that comprise the universal mantra written "om" in the roman alphabet and *aun* in Japanese.

Parrots are counted *ichiwa* 一羽.

● おうむ返し   *ōmugaeshi*   "a parrot's refrain"
parrot, regurgitate, echo (what someone says)

○ 彼女は緊張のあまり、面接官の質問をオウム返しするばかりだった。

   Kanojo wa kinchō no amari, mensetsu-kan no shitsumon o ōmu-gaeshi suru bakari datta.

   She was so nervous all she could do was repeat the interviewer's questions.

○ うちの娘は親の言うことをオウム返しするので下手なこと言えない。

   Uchi no musume wa oya no iu koto o ōmugaeshi suru no de heta na koto ienai.

   My daughter parrots everything she hears at home, so we have to watch what we say.

おしどり （鴛鴦） *oshidori* mandarin duck

☞ Often seen in pairs, especially during the winter in Japan, this beautiful crested Asian duck is considered a symbol of conjugal affection, harmony, and fidelity in China as well as Japan, where it is common in shady ponds and lakes. In truth, however, these ducks change partners every year, only slightly less often than daytime Japanese TV would have contemporary housewives slip under the sheets with hard-working hubby's friends.

Mandarin ducks are counted *ichiwa* 一羽.

● おしどり夫婦　*oshidori-fūfu*　"Mandarin duck man and wife"

a happily married couple, a couple of (married) lovebirds, two people whose marriage was made in heaven

○ 佐々木さんはおしどり夫婦で有名だ。
Sasaki-san wa oshidori-fūfu de yūmei da.
The Sasakis are notorious as a happily married couple.

○ おしどり夫婦で通っていたあのタレント夫婦の突然の離婚で、芸能雑誌が騒いでいる。
Oshidori-fūfu de tōtte ita ano tarento-fūfu no totsuzen no rikon de, geinō-zasshi ga sawaide iru.
The tabloids are going crazy now, what with the marriage of those two stars on the rocks, when everyone thought they were a couple of lovebirds.

✌ From the mistaken belief that mandarin ducks mate for life.

かも（鴨）　*kamo*　wild duck

☞ Of the approximately thirty or so species known to visit Japan, all but a few are migratory. The lucky ones winter in the nation's lakes and rivers before returning north in the spring; the unlucky ones end up in a variety of delectable dishes, including *kamonabe* 鴨鍋, or duck soup.

Ducks are considered to be easy marks in much the same way an English speaker would think of pigeons, presumably because they are good hunting.

Ducks are counted *ichiwa* 一羽.

● 鴨（いい鴨）　*kamo (ii kamo)*　"a duck (good duck)"

a pigeon, sucker, dupe, patsy; an easy mark

○ おい見ろ、鴨が向こうから歩いてきたぞ。
Oi miro, kamo ga mukō kara aruite kita zo.
Check out that pigeon coming this way.

○ お前は人がいいから、キャッチセールスのたぐいのいい鴨なんだよ。
Omae wa hito ga ii kara, kyatchi-sērusu no tagui no ii kamo nan da yo.
You're too nice for your own good. Somebody like those guys selling stuff on street corners is gonna take you to the cleaners some day.

🐇 From the notion that ducks are slow to get airborn and thus easy marks for hunters.

● 鴨にする　*kamo ni suru*
sucker *someone,* make a patsy out of *someone*

○ 今度加納を麻雀に誘って鴨にしてやろう。
Kondo Kanō o mājan ni sassotte kamo ni shite yarō.
I'm gonna get Kano to play some mah-jongg with us next time and clean him out.

○ この前はポーカーでいい鴨にされたよ。
Kono mae wa pōkā de ii kamo ni sareta yo.
They saw me coming the other day when I played poker. / I got suckered (duped) into playing poker the other day.

● 鴨が葱を背負ってくる　*kamo ga negi o shotte kuru*　"a duck coming (to dinner) with a load of leeks on its back" more than *one* can ask (hope) for, a dream come true; *someone* just asking for it

---

○ 育児でヘトヘトになっているとき、たまたま親がおむつを持って来たんで、思わず「鴨か葱を背負って来た」と心の中で叫んだね。
Ikuji de hetoheto ni natte iru toki, tamatama oya ga omutsu o motte kita n' de omowazu "Kamo ga negi o shotte kita" to kokoro no naka de sakenda ne.
Just as I was about worn to a frazzle from looking after the baby, Mother came visiting with a bunch of diapers. I could hardly keep from crying out, "What a godsend!"

○ 借金返済に困っているところに弟が宝くじに当たったと駆け込んできたんだから、まさに「鴨葱」だった。
Shakkin-hensai ni komatte iru tokoro ni otōto ga takarakuji ni atatta to kakekonde kita n' da kara, masa ni "kamo-negi" datta.
Just as I was wondering how to pay off this loan, my kid brother came prancing in, saying he won at the lottery. Well, what more could you ask for.

🐇 At the very minimum, two things are necessary to prepare *kamo nabe* 鴨鍋, or duck soup: a duck and some leeks. So it's just too good to be true when a duck comes waddling up with those very same leeks on his back, just when your gastric juices are starting to flow. This phrase is often given in abbreviated form: *kamo-negi.*

● 鴨の水掻き　*kamo no mizukaki*　"a duck's paddling"
unappreciated or unnoticed hard work; toil (done) in obscurity

---

○ 自営業は気楽に見えるかも知れないがその実鴨の水掻きです。
Jieigyō wa kiraku ni mieru kamo shirenai ga sono jitsu kamo no mizukaki desu.
It may look like a carefree way to make a living, but there's a lot of unseen hard work that goes into being in business for yourself.

○ 彼は会社でやり手に見られているが、実際は鴨の水掻きなんじゃ
ないのかなあ。
Kare wa kaisha de yarite ni mirarete iru ga, jissai wa kamo no mizukaki nan ja nai no ka nā.
At the office he's got a reputation for being a fast worker, but I can't help thinking that behind the scenes he's got his nose to the grindstone.

❧ From the observation that while ducks may look like they are tooling along effortlessly in the water, in fact they are paddling away like mad under the surface.

からす（烏）　*karasu*　CROW

☞ This big, black, boisterous bird is an all too common sight and sound in the cities of Japan, where its cacophonous caw awakens entire neighborhoods, and its strong beak allow it to plunder the thin plastic garbage bags that line the streets every other weekday morning. Such characteristics have led this stout-billed bully—a "gregarious songbird" according to the dictionaries—to stand for a loud or coarse person, a loiterer, someone with disgusting table manners, or a scatterbrain. As if that were not bad enough, the crow's grating caw is generally held to presage bad news or the visitation of evil, and superstition once held that the future could be divined from its cry.

One word that has fallen into disuse but warrants mention here for its colorfulness is *karasugane* 烏金, or crow money, a high-interest, one-day loan that must be repaid early the next day when the crows start cawing, which is to say at daybreak.

The crow's caw is *kākā* カーカー. They are counted *ichiwa* 一羽.

● 烏合の衆　*ugō no shū*　"flock of crows"
a disorderly crowd, a gaggle, a herd of cats

○ 人数ばかり多くても烏合の衆では役に立たないよ。

Ninzū bakari ōkute mo ugō no shū de wa yaku ni tatanai yo.
No matter how many people you've got, they're useless if they're
just a milling crowd.

○ あんな弱いチームに負けたんじゃ、単なる烏合の衆といわれても
しかたがないよ。
*Anna yowai chīmu ni maketa n' ja, tan-naru ugō no shū to iwarete
mo shikata ga nai yo.*
If we can't beat a team as weak as that, we can't complain if we're
called a passel of good-for-nothings.

○ わが軍は単なる烏合の衆だ。
Wagagun wa tan-naru ugō no shū da.
Our army is nothing more than a ragtag bunch of rowdies.

⚐ Ever seen crows flying in formation? Neither have we. From the observation that crows are an unruly bunch.

● 烏の足跡　*karasu no ashiato*　"crow's footprints"
crow's-feet

○ あら、烏の足跡だわ。いやねぇ。
Ara, karasu no ashiato dawa. Iya nē.
My goodness! I've got crow's-feet around my eyes.

○ あの人烏の足跡があるからそんなに若くないよ。
Ano hito karasu no ashiato ga aru kara sonna ni wakaku nai yo.
He's got crow's-feet around his eyes, so he can't be all that young.

⚐ Exactly the same usage as in English. (And the same sinking feeling
seems to accompany first notice of them, too.)

● 烏の行水　*karasu no gyōzui*　"a crow's bath"
a hurried bath, a spit bath, a quick dip

○ 時間がなかったので烏の行水になった。
Jikan ga nakatta no de karasu no gyōzui ni natta.
I was short on time so I just made do with a spit bath.

○ 今風呂に入ったと思ったら、烏の行水だね。
Ima furo ni haitta to omottara, karasu no gyōzui da ne.
Boy, that was a quick bath. I could swear you just got in.

⚐ From the crow's hurried bathing habits.

● 三羽がらす　*sanba-garasu*　"three crows"

three people of ability; a triumvirate; the Big Three (of
something)

○ 三人はわが校、卓球部の三羽がらすと呼ばれている。

Sannin wa wagakō, takkyū-bu no sanba-garasu to yobarete iru.

They are known as the "Big Three" of our school's table tennis
team.

○ 陸上界の三羽がらすの一人と言われた彼女もその後は記録が伸び
なかった。

*Rikujō-kai no sanba-garasu no hitori to iwareta kanojo mo sono
go wa kiroku ga nobinakatta.*

Heralded as one of the top three stars of the track and field world,
she was unable thereafter to break her own record.

> がん（雁）　*gan*　wild goose

☞　These majestic, gregarious water birds come to Japan in the late fall
to stay until early spring, when they once again return north. Often living
in noisy flocks and known for their vigilance, geese can he found resting
on sandbars in rivers or on islands to gain a measure of protection from
their natural enemies, which include man. Given how long they have
been hunted here, one cannot but wonder why they continue to return.
The head of the traditional Japanese tobacco pipe, or *kiseru* きせる, and
other kinds of pipes are called *gankubi* 雁首, or goosenecks, from their
resemblance to the bird's head and neck when not outstretched in flight.
A similar observation has led to a peculiar type of American trailer hitch,
which mounts in the bed of a truck instead of on the rear bumper, being
called a "gooseneck."

Geese are known for their distinctive honk, which is *gangan* ガンガン.
They are counted *ichiwa* 一羽 or *ippiki* 一匹.

● 雁首そろえる　*gankubi soroeru*　"line up goose necks"

line up, form up

○ 何だ、兄弟三人雁首そろえて、小遣いでもねだりに来たのか。

*Nan da, kyōdai sannin gankubi soroete, kozukai de mo nedari ni
kita no ka.*

What's this? The three of you all lined up, thinking you're gonna
get your old dad to cough up some money?

○ 今部長が四人雁首そろえて社長室に入って行ったけど何かあった
のかなあ？

*Ima buchō ga yonin gankubi soroete shachō-shitsu ni haitte itta
   kedo nani ka atta no ka nā?*

I wonder what's up. All four department heads just marched into
   the president's office.

🦜 Possibly from the unique diagonal or "V" flying formations of these
migratory birds in which they line up their outstretched necks with near
perfection. A slang expression for head or neck, *gankubi* now appears almost exclusively in *gankubi o soroeru,* an often derogatory and sometimes jocular expression used of a limited number of people (as few as
two qualify) lining up for some specific purpose.

閑古鳥 *kankodori* cuckoo

☞ This is the old word for a cuckoo, which is more commonly known
today as a *kakkō* かっこう (郭公). Whatever it's called, and it is called
pretty much the same thing worldwide because of its distinctive cry
(*kakkōkakkō カッコウカッコウ*), this brazen migratory bird lays its eggs
in the nests of other unsuspecting birds and then merrily goes about its
business while its young are raised by surrogate—and unsuspecting—
parents.

● 閑古鳥が鳴く *kankodori ga naku* "the cuckoo cries"
business is slow (bad), the place is empty

○ 近ごろこの商店街でも閑古鳥が鳴いている。
   Chikagoro kono shōten-gai de mo kankodori ga naite iru.
   Even this shopping arcade (mall) has been dead (like a morgue)
      lately.

○ 今年は冷夏でどこのプールでも閑古鳥が鳴いている。
   Kotoshi wa reika de doko no pūru de mo kankodori ga naite iru.
   It's been so cold this summer that swimming pools are empty
      everywhere.

○ バブル経済も破綻して夜の銀座では閑古鳥が鳴きだした。
   *Baburu keizai mo hatan shite yoru no Ginza de wa kankodori ga
      nakidashita.*
   Now that the economic bubble has burst, the streets of the Ginza
      are all but deserted at night.

🦜 Perhaps from an association with the lonesome cry of the cuckoo in
quiet, remote areas. Referring to a lack of customers, visitors, or specta-
tors, this idiom can be used about shops, bars, museums, even sporting
events, practically anywhere money is made by selling services or prod-
ucts to customers.

きじ（雉）　*kiji*　pheasant

☞ This resident game bird, though seldom seen, makes its home in the foothills and fields of Japan, appears in such well-known Japanese folk tales as *Momotaro* 桃太郎, and was designated the national bird in 1947 (a little-known bit of trivia that might win you a couple of beers at the local *izakaya*). The idioms included here indicate that the bird's intelligence is not the characteristic that propelled it to become a national symbol. The high-pitched cry of pheasants—well, the males anyway, the one that gets them in trouble during the hunting season—is *kenkēn* ケンケーン. They are counted *ichiwa* 一羽.

● 雉も鳴かずば打たれまい　*kiji mo nakazuba utaremai*
"even a pheasant will not be shot if it remains quiet"
stay quiet and stay out of trouble

○ 「雉も鳴かずば打たれまい」ここはひとつじっと様子を見ていろ。
"Kiji mo nakazuba utaremai" koko wa hitotsu jitto yōsu o mite iro.
Let's just lay low for a while and see which way the wind blows.

○ この件については他言無用に願いますよ。雉も鳴かずば打たれまいというでしょう。
Kono ken ni tsuite wa tagon-muyō ni negaimasu yo. Kiji mo nakazuba utaremai to iu deshō.
We'd best keep this to ourselves (under our hats). You know what they say about loose lips sinking ships.

🐦 A graphic expression of inviting danger by drawing attention to oneself.

さぎ（鷺）　*sagi*　(snowy) heron

☞ These medium-sized water birds were formerly thought to be the cause of "balls of fire" seen flying through the night skies, and in a way they were. While they were not exactly breathing fire (some were actually called *hifukidori* 火吹き鳥, or fire-breathing birds), a certain species of heron was later discovered to have feathers that shine in the darkness. In this way, yet another of nature's wonderful mysteries was solved at the expense of our ability to marvel at the unknown.
Herons are counted *ichiwa* 一羽.

● 鷺を烏と言いくるめる　*sagi o karasu to iikurumeru*　"to insist that a heron is a crow"
talk black into white, twist everything to suit *oneself*

○ そういう鷺を烏と言いくるめるようなことを言っているから商売
にならないんだよ。

*Sō iu sagi o karasu to iikurumeru yō na koto o itte iru kara shōbai
ni naranai n' da yo.*

You're never going to make a go of it by saying things that fly in
the face of reason.

○ 彼女は鷺を烏と言いくるめる性格だから、困ったものだ。

*Kanojo wa sagi o karasu to iikurumeru seikaku da kara, komatta
mono da.*

The way she looks you straight in the eye and says that black is
white without cracking a smile is just too much.

🐰 From the obviously opposite colors and characteristics of the two
birds and the fact that the heron is held in higher esteem.

すずめ（雀）　*suzume*　sparrow

☞ They're everywhere, including some Japanese dinner tables. Not
that nouvelle cuisine is in, or dieting all the rage. No, they just eat sparrows butterflied and cooked over charcoal at some upscale eateries and
at some definitely downtown *yakitori-ya*s. If you can't manage to finish
off a Cornish game hen, then maybe a sparrow is right down your alley.
As a bonus, they are served head intact.

Sparrows figure in the language as metaphors for small things (some
diminutive or relatively small grasses and insects, for example, include
the character for "sparrow" in their names, usually indicating it is
smaller than other such species; the sparrow pea is smaller than the crow
pea). In yet another equally fascinating bit of trivia, a person who is always chattering away is called a "sparrow," as is a person who has the
inside dope on something and is not shy about sharing it. Such a chatter-
box is called a *gakuya suzume* 楽屋雀, or a backstage sparrow, from the
term's origin in the dressing rooms of Japanese theaters, where gossips
insinuated themselves and lived to tell all they had discovered about actors and actresses.

The sparrow's chirp is *chunchun* チュンチュン, and when there are a
lot of them going at it full blast in the trees, we have a *suzume-gassen* 雀
合戦, or a sparrow battle. When they sit still enough for a roll call, which
is rare, sparrows can be counted *ichiwa* 一羽 or *ippiki* 一匹.

● 雀の涙　*suzume no namida*　"a sparrow's tear"

a very small amount (of money), a piddling sum, a drop in
the bucket, next to nothing

○ 一日炎天下で働いて、報酬は雀の涙だった。

Ichinichi enten-ka de hataraite, hōshū wa suzume no namida datta.
Sweated my ass off in the hot sun all day for next to nothing.

○ 今どき、そんな雀の涙のようなバイト料で働く奴いないよ。
Imadoki, sonna suzume no namida no yō na baito-ryō de hataraku yatsu inai yo.
Nobody's going to take a part-time job these days for a piddling sum like that.

🦙 Used exclusively of money.

↪ *ka no namida* 蚊の涙

● 雀百まで踊り忘れず　*suzume hyaku made odori wasurezu*
"a sparrow can live to be a hundred and it won't forget how to dance"
old (bad) habits die hard; what is learned in the cradle is carried to the grave

---

○ 「雀百まで踊り忘れず」とよく言ったもので、この年になっても まだ部屋を暗くすると眠れません。
"Suzume hyaku made odori wasurezu" to yoku itta mono de, kono toshi ni natte mo mada heya o kuraku suru to nemuremasen.
They say old habits die hard, but I still can't get to sleep without having a light on, even at my age.

○ 私の息子は50歳にもなるのに、いまだになんでもやりっぱなし、 「雀百まで踊り忘れず」ですよ。
Watakushi no musuko wa gojū-sai ni mo naru no ni, imada ni nan de mo yarippanashi, "suzume hyaku made odori wasurezu" desu yo.
My son's going on fifty and he's still not acting his age (running wild). I guess it's true what they say about old habits dying hard.

🦙 The dancing here refers to the sparrow's proclivity to hop around, something it presumably does to the bitter end. The expression is primarily used of the bad habits one learns to enjoy early in life, often those born of a dissipated life of pleasure; wine, women (or men), and song.

たか（鷹）　*taka*　hawk

☞ Hawking and falconry have both been practiced in Japan since ancient times, when the sport was brought from Korea. Bravery, grace, and integrity, all positive characteristics, are associated with hawks. Yes, intransient hard-liners and war-mongers are hawks in Japanese too, as in *taka-ha* 鷹派, or hawk faction.

Hawks are counted *ichiwa* 一羽.

● 能ある鷹は爪を隠す　*nō aru taka wa tsume o kakusu*　"a powerful hawk hides its talons"

an able person does not show off his skills; tell not all you know, all you have, or all you can do

---

○ 能ある鷹は爪を隠す、ちょっとピアノが弾けるからって自慢するもんじゃないよ。

Nō aru taka wa tsume o kakusu, chotto piano ga hikeru kara tte jiman suru mon ja nai yo.

Don't toot your horn because you can play the piano a little. If you're good, people will discover it for themselves.

○ 能ある鷹は爪を隠すと言うけど、あの人がコンピュータプログラムが出来るとは知らなかった。

Nō aru taka wa tsume o kakusu to iu kedo, ano hito ga konpyūta puroguramu ga dekiru to wa shiranakatta.

I know what they say about ability being its own best advertisement, but what a surprise it was to find out that he knows how to program computers.

⚘ The opposite being equally true, it is to those who seek approbation for their modest abilities that this maxim is most often directed.

ちどり（千鳥）　*chidori*　plover

☞ The name *chidori* literally means "a thousand birds," and is thought to have come from the fact that the wee riparians are usually seen in large flocks. Twelve of the world's sixty or so species of plovers can be found in Japan's marshlands and along its shores. Unlike its three-toed namesakes, which are known to be vigorous walkers, the five-toed variety, often sighted primarily during hours of darkness in towns and cities across the nation, seems to have an inordinate amount of difficulty ambulating, particularly in a straight line. Plovers, considered winter birds in Japan, are counted *ichiwa* 一羽.

● 千鳥足　*chidoriashi*　"plover legs"

wobbly (rubbery) legs

○ 飲み過ぎたその客は千鳥足で店を出て行った。

Nomisugita sono kyaku wa chidoriashi de mise o dete itta.
The tipsy patron staggered out of the joint on rubbery legs.

○ 千鳥足だったから家に着くのにいつもの倍かかったよ。
Chidoriashi datta kara ie ni tsuku no ni itsumo no bai kakatta yo.
With my legs feeling like rubber bands, it took me twice as long as usual to get home.

⅋ Used primarily of the way a drunk walks, from the manner in which the plover crosses its legs one over the other as it darts about in search of a meal. Research has shown that the plover's unique walk is, in fact, a ploy which allows it to catch unsuspecting prey.

つばめ（燕）*tsubame* swallow

☞ This auspicious migratory bird comes to Japan each spring from Southeast Asia, and most return when the weather turns cold. Swallows are considered to herald the arrival of spring, where many consider a swallow's nest under the eaves of their home a sign that the household will prosper. In appreciation for having one's house selected by swallows as a nesting place, some families even place small shell amulets in the nest, believing that they will guarantee the safe birth of children. Swallows are counted *ichiwa* 一羽.

● 若い燕 *wakai tsubame* "a young swallow"
a young male lover, a gigilo

○ あの中年女優は若い燕と同棲している。
Ano chūnen-joyū wa wakai tsubame to dōsei shite iru.
That middle-aged actress is shacking up with some young stud.

○ 京子最近若い燕ができたらしいわよ。
Kyōko saikin wakai tsubame ga dekita rashii wa yo.
It looks like Kyoko's found herself a young bohunk.

⅋ Of a young man who has attached himself to an older woman and is usually kept by her as a lover. Said to have originated during the Meiji period when a famous woman's rights activist received a letter written by a painter (to whom she was later married by common law), in which he referred to himself as a *wakai tsubame*.

つる（鶴）*tsuru* crane

☞ Known for its grace and beauty, the crane has long been revered in Japan as a sacred bird that embodied a divine spirit and transported it to

Japan's shores from distant lands. Folk legend throughout Japan has the crane bringing rice cultivation to Japan from the north, and the bird's yearly arrival in winter is a newsworthy event that prompts television reports and specials even today.

Japanese folk legend also associates the crane with the weather. It is thought that the bird, craning its neck upward with a whoop, signals blue skies ahead, and looking down, conversely, rain.

Finally, as can be seen from the phrase *tsuru wa sennen kame wa mannen* 鶴は千年亀は万年, cranes, like turtles, are thought to have extremely long lifespans, and dreaming of them, therefore, is believed to guarantee that the dreamer will enjoy a long life.

Cranes are counted *ichiwa* 一羽.

● 千羽鶴　*senbazuru*　"a thousand cranes"
a thousand folded-paper cranes (on a string)

○ 則男君のお見舞いにみんなで千羽鶴を折りましょう。
Norio-kun no omimai ni minna de senbazuru o orimashō.
Let's all make a chain of paper cranes for when we go to see Norio in the hospital.

○ 千羽鶴は折り紙の中で一番ポピュラーだと思うよ。
Senbazuru wa origami no naka de ichiban popyurā da to omou yo.
Crane chains are the most popular type of origami, I'd say.

❦ As can be seen from the examples, *senbazuru* are folded and attached to a string to express one's hopes for success in a specific endeavor or the speedy recovery of an ill or injured person. They are sent or given directly to the person to whom one's good wishes are directed or may be hung at Shinto shrines, where they represent the earnest prayers of the makers.

● 鶴の一声　*tsuru no hitokoe*　"the single cry of a crane"
a word from on high, the voice of authority; one's word is law

---

○ 社長の鶴の一声でその計画は実行に移った。
Shachō no tsuru no hitokoe de sono keikaku wa jikkō ni utsutta.
One word from the boss and the plan was implemented.

○ やっぱりお前の鶴の一声がないとみんな動かないよ。
Yappari omae no tsuru no hitokoe ga nai to minna ugokanai yo.
You know, nobody's going to make a move until you give the go-ahead.

❦ In Japan, authority has the last word, especially when the small fry are at loggerheads over how to proceed or in an otherwise confused state. The logjam is broken when someone whose word is law finally speaks.

とび／とんび（鳶） *to(n)bi* kite

☞ As may be garnered from one of the entries included below, these slender, graceful hawks are one rung down on the linguistic ledger from their usually larger cousins. They make their homes near human habitations or the ocean and circle high above, searching for the carrion upon which they often feed.

Their high-pitched cry is *pīhyororo* ピーヒョロロ. They are counted *ichiwa* 一羽.

● 鳶が鷹を生む *tobi (tonbi) ga taka o umu* "a kite gives birth to a hawk"
parents may have children who are much better than they are

○ あの人の子が東大に入るなんて、鳶が鷹を生んだんだよそれは。
Ano hito no ko ga Tōdai ni hairu nante, tonbi ga taka o unda n' da yo sore wa.
His kid's getting into Tokyo University shows that anybody can have a genius in the family.

○ 鳶が鷹を生むっていうけど、あの八百屋の娘はまさにそれだ。
Tonbi ga taka o umu tte iu kedo, ano yaoya no musume wa masani sore da.
That greengrocer's daughter is living proof that kids can turn out better than their parents.

⚐ From the notion that a kite is lesser than other hawks comes this notion that an ordinary couple can have extraordinary children.

↝ *kaeru no ko wa kaeru* 蛙の子は蛙

● 鳶職 *tobishoku* "kite work"
construction work; a construction worker, a hardhat, (especially) a steeplejack

---

○ 俺の親父は鳶職で、若い頃に一度大けがして命拾いしてるんだ。
Ore no oyaji wa tobishoku de, wakai koro ni ichido ōkega shite inochi-biroi shiteru n' da.
My old man's a hardhat, 'n once he almost got killed on the job.

○ 最近は3Kなどといわれて、鳶職が少なくなっている。

Saikin wa san-kei nado to iwarete, tobishoku ga sukunaku natte iru.

With the aversion lately for difficult, dangerous, and dirty work, there are fewer and fewer people willing to work high up in scaffolding.

✌ Of construction workers, especially when their duties take them high up on scaffolding. Also *tobi no mono* 鳶の者 or simply *tobi* 鳶. Formerly of firemen, men involved in the moving of logs, as well as construction workers, the appellation arises from the fact that men doing such work carried pike-like fire hooks or other sharply hooked poles that resembled the kite's beak.

● 鳶に油揚げをさらわれる   *to(n)bi ni aburaage o sarawareru* "to have the deep-fried bean curd carried off by a kite" have something stolen that was almost in *one's* hand , have *one's* share snatched away at the last moment

---

○ 鳶に油揚げをさらわれるというけどまさか親友に彼女を取られるとは思わなかった。

Tonbi ni aburaage o sarawareru to iu kedo masaka shin'yū ni kanojo o torareru to wa omowanakatta.

Who would have ever thought that such a close friend would up and steal my girl.

○ ダントツで首位だったドライバーが最終周でエンジントラブル、2位が優勝して、鳶に油揚げをさらわれた形になった。

Dantotsu de shui datta doraibā ga saishū-shū de enjin toraburu, nii ga yūshō shite, tonbi ni aburaage o sarawareta katachi ni natta.

After being way out in front, he snatched defeat from the jaws of victory by losing to the number two car when engine trouble forced him to drop out on the last lap.

✌ Of things, thought to have been uncontestably one's own, being stolen by someone else, usually at the last minute.

とり（鳥） *tori* bird

☞ The generic word for feathered fellows of all kinds, *tori* is also used to mean chicken or pheasant, and *tori niku* 鳥 肉 is the word for "chicken," as in "meat" or "fowl."

● 立つ鳥跡を濁さず　*tatsu tori ato o nigosazu*　"birds taking to flight leave nothing sullied behind"
clean up a place before *one* leaves, leave a place like *one* found it

○ ちゃんと掃除してから帰りなさい、立つ鳥跡を濁さずと言うでしょう。
Chanto sōji shite kara kaerinasai, tatsu tori ato o nigosazu to iu deshō.
Clean up before you leave. You know what they say about leaving a place like you found it.

○ 花見の季節の上野公園のゴミは十数トンにのぼる、立つ鳥跡を濁さずは鳥の世界だけのものになってしまった。
Hanami no kisetsu no Ueno-kōen no gomi wa jūsū ton ni noboru, tatsu tori ato o nigosazu wa tori no sekai dake no mono ni natte shimatta.
The way they have to collect more than a dozen tons of garbage in Ueno Park when the cherry blossom viewing season winds down, it makes you think that the old adage about cleaning up after yourself has gone out the window.

⚓ From the notion that waterfowl do not leave the water befowled upon flying off. Used as an exhortation to leave a place the way one found it.

● 飛ぶ鳥を落とす勢い　*tobu tori o otosu ikioi*　"powerful enough to bring down a bird in flight"
high-flying, very energetic, vigorous; powerful; influential

○ 彼は飛ぶ鳥を落とす勢いで出世した。
Kare wa tobu tori o otosu ikioi de shusse shita.
He practically shot to the top. / He got on the fast track and went right to the top.

○ 飛ぶ鳥を落とす勢いだった日本車の輸出も今では昔話になりつつある。
Tobu tori o otosu ikioi datta Nihonsha no yushutsu mo ima de wa mukashibanashi ni naritsutsu aru.
The Japanese auto export juggernaut is well on its way to being a thing of the past.

⚓ Perhaps from the notion that it requires a great deal of speed for a projectile to hit and kill a bird on the wing.

● 鳥肌が立つ　*torihada ga tatsu*　"chicken skin stands"
get goose bumps (goose pimples, gooseflesh)

○ 寒いな、ほら見てよ、鳥肌が立ってるよ。
Samui na, hora mite yo, torihada ga tatte 'ru yo.
Burr, it's cold. Just look, I've got goosebumps all over.

○ 昨夜のコンサートは鳥肌が立つほど感動した。
Sakuya no konsāto wa torihada ga tatsu hodo kandō shita.
Last night's concert was so great that it actually gave me goose pimples.

⚘ Metaphoric use about how cold, fearful, or exciting something may be; usually expressed by adding ～ような. Examples of this use follow:

● 鳥肌が立つような　*torihada ga tatsu yō na*　"enough to make chicken skin stand"
cold (frightening, exciting) enough to give *one* goosebumps

○ 鳥肌が立つようなぞっとする光景を目の当たりにして、彼は身動きひとつできなかった。
Torihada ga tatsu yō na zotto suru kōkei o ma no atari ni shite, kare wa miugoki hitotsu dekinakatta.
He stood there unable to move as the horrific sight unfolded before him.

○ 今日は鳥肌が立つような寒さだなあ。
Kyō wa torihada ga tatsu yō na samusa da nā.
Jeez, it's cold enough to give you goosepimples today.

● 鳥目　*torime*　"bird eyes"
night blindness, nyctalopia; a night-blind person

○ 私は鳥目です。
Watashi wa torime desu.
I am night blind. / I can't see at night.

○ 鳥目の彼女は交差点の向こうにいるボーイフレンドに気づかなかった。
Torime no kanojo wa kōsaten no mukō ni iru bōifurendo ni kizukanakatta.
She was so night blind that she couldn't even make out her boyfriend, who was just across the intersection.

⚯ From the observation that the majority of birds do not see well at night, this slang term for the medical condition is most commonly used of people who just have trouble seeing in the dark. Jocular, it is rarely used for the actual medical condition.

● 鳥 も 通 わ ぬ   *tori mo kayowanu*   "even birds don't frequent"
isolated, remote, deserted

○ その寺は鳥も通わぬ山奥にあった。
Sono tera wa tori mo kayowanu yamaoku ni atta.
The remote temple was situated deep in the mountains.

○ 人との接触を嫌ったその老人は鳥も通わぬ離れ小島で余生を送った。
Hito to no sesshoku o kiratta sono rōjin wa tori mo kayowanu hanare-kojima de yosei o okutta.
Wanting nothing to do with human beings, the old man spent his remaining years on an isolated outlying island.

⚯ From the notion that if not even birds, which seem to be just about everywhere, aren't around, a place must be way out in the sticks. It is used adjectivally of remote places.

とり／にわとり（鶏）*tori/niwatori* chicken

☞ This common barnyard fowl figures in few idioms, none of which indicate it is held in any particular esteem in Japan. In general, compounds incorporating the character for chicken display the disdain in which this lowly yardbird is held. *Keikan* 鶏姦, literally "chicken rape," is a literary term for sodomy or pederasty, presumably from this barnyard fowl's indiscriminate amorousness. *Keigun* 鶏群, literally "a flock of chickens," is another literary term for a bunch of people raising a ruckus over nothing. From this term comes the idiom *keigun no ikkaku* 鶏群の一鶴, literally "a crane among chickens," that describes a person of superior qualities who stands out among surrounding pedestrian types. *Keikō* 鶏口, or chicken mouth, is a term to describe the head of a small group. It figures in the idiom *keikō to naru mo gyūgo to naru nakare* 鶏口となるも牛後となる勿れ, literally "become a chicken's mouth, not a cow's butt." Loosely translated it means something like "better a big fish in a small pond than a small fish in a big one," though it is more accurately rendered as "better to lead a small group than follow in a large one." And finally, *keiroku* 鶏肋, "a chicken's breastbone," plays on the notion that while the amount of meat on a breastbone may not be much, it is just enough to make it difficult to throw away, and produces the metaphorical meaning of something or someone that is not particularly useful but doesn't quite warrant being gotten rid of. It can also mean a small, weak body.

● 風見鶏 *kazamidori* "a bird that looks at the wind"
a weathercock, an opportunist, an unprincipled person who follows the majority

---

○ あいつは風見鶏だから同僚からは信頼されていない。
Aitsu wa kazamidori da kara dōryō kara wa shinrai sarete inai.
The guy's such an opportunist that none of his co-workers trust him.

○ 昔風見鶏と言われた日本の首相がいたが、その後政治スキャンダルで辞任した。
Mukashi kazamidori to iwareta Nihon no shushō ga ita ga, sono go seiji sukyandaru de jinin shita.
A long time ago there used to be a Japanese prime minister that everybody called the weathercock, but he resigned because of some political scandal.

⚘ This bird (*tori*) is really a chicken (*niwatori*). But the character can be pronounced *tori,* and is, in fact, so pronounced at meat markets all around the country. Ask for *toriniku,* or bird meat, and you'll get chicken and not sparrow or pheasant. The weathervane usage is similar to the English and derives from the similarity of such a person to the erratic gyrations of the figurine atop buildings. Roosters make the sound *koke-kokkō* コケコッコウ.

| はと （鳩） *hato* pigeon or dove |

☞ This municipal scourge is as prevalent in Japanese cities as anywhere else, especially around train stations, under overpasses, and in parks. The far more beautiful wild dove is, unfortunately, far less common. Still it symbolizes peace and prosperity in Japan as elsewhere. And yes, those peace-loving folks who are always willing to try to see the other guy's side of things are doves in Japanese, too. And as with their natural enemies the hawks, *-ha* 〜派 is attached to describe them as a faction.

The coo of doves and pigeons is *poppo* ポッポ. In baby talk, both pigeons and their coo are *poppo*. They are counted *ichiwa* 一羽.

● 鳩首 *kyūshu* "dove (or pigeon) necks"
get together to discuss something, put *ones'* heads together, huddle (up)

○ 経営陣は不況対策で鳩首会議をしているところだ。
Keieijin wa fukyō-taisaku de kyūshu-kaigi o shite iru tokoro da.
The big wigs are in the middle of a powwow, trying to figure out a way to cope with the recession.

○ 首相のスキャンダル打開のため与党の幹部が鳩首密議を始めた。
Shushō no sukyandaru dakai no tame yotō no kanbu ga kyūshu-mitsugi o hajimeta.
Top-ranking members of the government (party in power) put their heads together to find a way out of the scandal swirling around the prime minister.

⚘ From the observation that pigeons congregate comes this expression for a number of people getting together to discuss something.

● 鳩が豆鉄砲を食ったような *hato ga mamedeppō o kutta yō na* "like a pigeon that has just been hit by a pea shooter" astounded, astonished, blown-away, floored

---

○ なんだそんな鳩が豆鉄砲を食ったような顔して。
Nan da sonna hato ga mamedeppō o kutta yō na kao shite.
What are you looking so flabbergasted about?

○ 死んだはずの夫が帰ってきたので、妻は鳩が豆鉄砲を食ったような顔で言葉も出ず立ち尽くした。
Shinda hazu no otto ga kaette kita no de, tsuma wa hato ga mame-deppō o kutta yō na kao de kotoba mo dezu tachitsukushita.
Dumbfounded, she just stood there open-mouthed when her supposedly dead husband suddenly turned up.

⚘ Of the wide-eyed expression imagined to resemble that of a pigeon that has just been hit by a beanshooter. Not used about dangerous or life-threatening situations.

ふくろう（梟） *fukurō* owl

☞ This usually nocturnal carnivore is common in the forests of Japan but appears to have never inspired the notions of wisdom or omniscience that are commonly attributed to its Western counterparts. Its only characteristic worthy of lingiustic note in Japanese appears to be its activity at night, a trait it shares with owls everywhere. The protrusions on its head, by the way, are tufts of feathers, not ears, though they are sometimes called that.
The owl's cry is variously *hōhō* ホウホウ or *gorosukehohho* ゴロスケ

ホッホ. They are counted *ippiki* 一匹 or *ichiwa* 一羽.

● ふくろう （梟） *fukurō* owl
  a nightowl, a person who stays up late, a night person

○ そんなふくろうみたいな生活してると体こわすよ。
  Sonna fukurō mitai na seikatsu shite 'ru to karada kowasu yo.
  You'll ruin your health living like a nightowl like that.

○ 彼女がふくろうのような仕事をしているのは、誰にも言わないが
  大きな夢があるらしい。
  *Kanojo ga fukurō no yō na shigoto o shite iru no wa, dare ni mo
  iwanai ga ōki na yume ga aru rashii.*
  She doesn't let on to anybody, but the reason she's working till all
  hours of the night is that she's pursuing a dream of hers.

✌ From the owl's nocturnal habits.

4

魚介類
FISH AND SHELLFISH

Fish and shellfish have long been a major source of pro-
tein for the Japanese. Hey, Japan is a bunch of islands
surrounded by the plenty of the oceans that lap upon its
shores. But while Westerners have gradually awakened to the
health benefits of seafood, many Japanese seem bent on undoing their own low incidence of clogged arteries and heart failure and plunging headlong into a diet replete with animal fats.

Centuries of fishermen bobbing around on the seas, however, have placed fish and mollusks on the linguistic menu
in great numbers and variety. From the fact that *medaka*, or
killifish, small freshwater bait fish often used for mosquito
abatement, inhabit streams in schools comes the idiomatic expression *medaka no gakkō* メダカの学校 for a group of small
children. *Fugu*, or puffers, fish that can be prepared only by
licensed chefs in Japan because of a poisonous liver that can
prove fatal when eaten, figure in the expression *fugu wa
kuitashi inochi wa oshishi* フグは食いたし命は惜しし, remark-
ing on the difficulty one has making up his mind to do something dangerous.

あわび（鮑） *awabi* abalone

☞ This increasingly less common shellfish lends its moniker to the lexicon of love from the observation that although it is a true univalve, it appears to be a bivalve missing one of its two shells and is, hence, in search
of its other (better?) half. It is otherwise lexically undistinguished.

Awabi are counted *ichimai* 一枚.

● 鮑の片思い *awabi no kataomoi* "an abalone's one-sided love"

unrequited love, one-sided love, carrying a (the) torch for *someone*

○ 佳子さんの片思い、もう3年にもなるんだって。
Yoshiko-san no kataomoi, mō sannen ni mo naru n' datte.
They say Yoshiko's been carrying the torch for three long years.

○ おまえはいつも鮑の片思いだなあ。どうしてもてないんだろう。
Omae wa itsumo awabi no kataomoi da nā. Dōshite motenai n' darō.
You're always in love with some chick that doesn't even know you're alive. Wonder why you can't find yourself a woman.

✌ *Awabi* is often deleted from the expression altogether.

いわし（鰯） *iwashi* sardine

☞ Appreciation for this lowly regarded but always numerous plebe of the oceans is growing as other more highly prized delectables vanish from the plundered seas. Sardines, fresh or preserved in salt, have been eaten as common fare by Japanese for centuries and figure in several idioms expressive of numerousness or the color gray. A dull sword was known as an *iwashi*, perhaps because of its namesake's slender, silvery body (which isn't much good for cutting anything), and a rusted sword was called an *akaiwashi*, from the red hue the salted sardine takes on. The fact that *iwashi* expire almost immediately after being removed from water is part of their image in the Japanese mind (note that the right side of character for *iwashi* means "weak").

● いわし雲 *iwashigumo* "sardine cloud"

a small, white, fleecy cloud; a cirrocumulus; a mackerel cloud; (of a sky in which such clouds appear) a mackerel sky

○ 今日はいわし雲が出ていた。
Kyō wa iwashigumo ga dete ita.
There was a mackerel sky today.

○ 真冬にいわし雲とは珍しいな。
Mafuyu ni iwashigumo to wa mezurashii na.

It's unusual for there to be these small, fleecy clouds in winter-time.

𝔖 Colloquial word for such clouds. Closely tied to autumn, their mention brings to mind that season. There are apparently two theories of the word's origin, one based on the notion that such cloud formations resemble schooling sardines, the other that ancient fishermen believed that the appearance of such clouds signaled a large catch of sardines. The formations were also thought to portend heavy rain and winds, a meteorologically sound observation since these clouds, which form high in the troposphere, are often the high-level blowoff of deeper precipitating clouds farther upwind. They are, according to meteorologist R. A. Rangno, "the smoke from the fire."

うお／さかな（魚）　*uo/sakana*　fish

☞ The generic word for things that swim, have gills, and seldom venture out on rollerblades. Fish like salmon that return to spawn in rivers where they were born are newly released in the streams and rivers of Japan to check the advance or abatement of pollution. Oddly enough, with regard to the human world, the expression *mizu kiyokereba uo sumazu* 水清ければ魚棲まず, literally, fish do not dwell in pure water, is used to express the idea that a person who is too principled is unlikely to be accepted by others.

● 魚心あれば水心あり　*uogokoro areba mizugokoro ari*　"if the fish feels that way, so will the water"
scratch my back and I'll scratch yours; logrolling

○ 魚心あれば水心ありで、責任は誘った男だけじゃなく、誘われた女にもあるさ。
Uogokoro areba mizugokoro aride, sekinin wa sasotta otoko dake ja naku, sasowareta onna ni mo aru sa.
Responsibility lies not just with the man who tempted the woman, but also with the woman who allowed herself to be tempted. After all, it takes two to tango.

○ 魚心あれば水心あり、その会社は富士商事の商談に乗った。
Uogokoro areba mizugokoro ari, sono kaisha wa Fuji-shōji no shōdan ni notta.
Seeing that there was something in it for both parties, the company took Fuji Trading up on its offer.

𝔖 From a sense of mutuality between two entities, usually with both parties feeling positively about the other. And, yes, there's something fishy going on behind the scenes here, too.

● 雑魚　*zako*　"various fish"
small fish; small fry

○ 今日は雑魚ばかり釣れた。
Kyō wa zako bakari tsureta.
I just caught a bunch of garbage (small) fish today.

○ 雑魚は相手にせず、大物だけを狙え。
Zako wa aite ni sezu, ōmono dake o nerae.
Don't bother with the small fry, go for the big wigs.

○ 警察は大がかりな摘発作戦に出たが、検挙したのは雑魚ばかりだった。
Keisatsu wa ōgakari na tekihatsu-sakusen ni deta ga, kenkyo shita no wa zako bakari datta.
The police began a large-scale roundup of criminals, but ended up netting a bunch of small-time crooks.

● 雑魚寝　*zako-ne*　"sleep together like various fish"
sleep together in a huddle

○ 旅行社の手違いで、小さな部屋に他の客と一緒に雑魚寝させられた。
Ryokō-sha no techigai de, chiisana heya ni hoka no kyaku to issho ni zako-ne saserareta.
Thanks to a slip-up on the tour company's part, we had to sleep all huddled up with other guests in one room.

○ その不法入国者達は6畳のアパートに雑魚寝しているところを検挙された。
Sono fuhō-nyūkokusha-tachi wa roku-jō no apāto ni zako-ne shite iru tokoro o kenkyo sareta.
When the illegal immigrants were picked up, they were all sleeping packed into one six-mat room.

✍ From the hodgepodge of small fish landed in nets. Often used of men and women sleeping huddled together in one room.

● 白魚のような指　*shirauo no yō na yubi*　"fingers like white fish"
delicate white fingers

○ 彼女は白魚のような指をしていた。

Kanojo wa shirauo no yō na yubi o shite ita.
She had delicate white fingers.

○ 白魚のような指の彼女には、真珠の指輪がぴったりだ。

Shirauo no yō na yubi no kanojo ni wa, shinju no yubiwa ga pittari da.

A pearl ring is perfect for a woman like her with beautiful, long white fingers.

🐚 This colorless, semitransparent fish is about four inches in length and, unlike fingers, is eaten in Japan. Idiomatic usage derives from the fish's fanciful resemblance to a finger and the traditional Japanese aesthetic which dictates that white skin, especially on women, is desirable.

● 逃がした魚は大きい　*nigashita sakana wa ōkii*　"the uncaught fish is big"

the one that got away, it's always the biggest fish that gets away

---

○ 逃がした魚は大きいと言うが、別れて初めて彼女のすばらしさに気づいたよ。

Nigashita sakana wa ookii to iu ga, wakarete hajimete kanojo no subarashisa ni kizuita yo.

That say the biggest one always gets away, and it was only after we had broken up that I realized what a wonderful person she is.

○ あの人の自慢話は大分差し引いて聞かなければいけない「逃がした魚は大きい」というでしょう。

Ano hito no jiman-banashi wa daibu sashihiite kikanakereba naranai "Nigashita sakana wa ookii" to iu deshō.

You have to take everything he says with a grain of salt. It's always "the big one got away" with him.

● 水を得た魚　*mizu o eta uo*　"a fish (back) in water"
back in *one's* element

○ 転職して、いまの彼女は水を得た魚だね。

Tenshoku shite, ima no kanojo wa mizu o eta uo da ne.

Changing jobs has done wonders for her.

○ 彼は水を得た魚のように、元の部署に戻ってからはその能力を発揮した。

Kare wa mizu o eta uo no yō ni, moto no busho ni modotte kara wa sono nōryoku o hakki shita.

Upon returning to his former section, he was back in his element and soon showing what he could do.

❦ The opposite of the English "like a fish out of water," this idiom describes a change in surroundings that breathe new life into someone who has previously suffered.

•➤ *mizu o hanareta uo* 水を離れた魚

● 水を離れた魚 *mizu o hanareta uo* "a fish away from water"
(be) like a fish out of water, out of one's element

○ 父は定年退職してまるで水を離れた魚状態になってしまった。
Chichi wa teinen-taishoku shite maru de mizu o hanareta uo jōtai ni natte shimatta.
Dad was just like a fish out of water when he retired.

○ 人事移動で営業をはずされた彼は水を離れた魚のようになってしまった。
Jinji-idō de eigyō o hazusareta kare wa mizu o hanareta uo no yō ni natte shimatta.
Reassignment within the company left him high and dry, his connections to the sales department severed.

❦ Also (though less commonly) used in the reshuffled form *uo no mizu ni hanareta yō* 魚の水に離れたよう.

•➤ *mizu o eta uo* 水を得た魚

（うなぎ）鰻 *unagi* eel

☞ Though its fry are born in the ocean, the Japanese eel is considered a freshwater fish because it swims up streams and rivers to live. Eels have long been considered nutritious and are eaten on the eighteenth day of July by many Japanese in the hope that doing so will protect them from getting sick during the summer. Eels are counted *ippiki* 一匹 or *ippon* 一本.

● 鰻の寝床 *unagi no nedoko* "an eel's bed"
a long, narrow place to sleep or live; a sliver of land

○ 派手な生活をしている中村さんも家に帰れば鰻の寝床のようなボロ家住まいだ。

Hade na seikatsu o shite iru Nakamura-san mo ie ni kaereba unagi no nedoko no yō na boroya-zumai da.

Nakamura may have a flashy lifestyle, but he goes home to a cramped dump at night.

○ 被災地では、仮設住宅が鰻の寝床のように並んでいる。

Hisai-chi de wa, kasetsu-jūtaku ga unagi no nedoko no yō ni narande iru.

Rows of barracks have been thrown up in the disaster area to provide temporary shelter.

○ こんな鰻の寝床みたいな土地じゃ店舗には向かないな。

Konna unagi no nedoko mitai na tochi ja tenpo ni wa mukanai na.

A sliver of land like this (with almost no frontage) won't do for a business. / You could never make a business work on a strip of land like this, with almost no frontage.

⚘ Of land, buildings, or rooms. From the observation that eels, being eels, need a long but not a wide place to sleep.

● 鰻登り *unagi nobori* "eel climbing"
skyrocket, soar, take off, go out of sight

○ 新製品の人気はまさに鰻登りだ。

Shin-seihin no ninki wa masa ni unagi nobori da.

The popularity of the new product is simply soaring. / The new product is really taking off.

○ 天候不順で、野菜の値段が鰻登りに上がっている。

Tenkō-fujun de, yasai no nedan ga unagi nobori ni agatte iru.

Vegetable prices are skyrocketing due to the bad weather.

⚘ Used primarily of such things as prices, which are expressed in numbers. According to one source the expression derives from the eel's manner of rising quickly in the water, while a second source claims it is from the eel's slippery climb up and out of your hands—and control—when you try to grasp it.

えび（海老） *ebi* shrimp / prawn / lobster

☞ Among these auspicious crustaceans, lobsters are often served on commemorative occasions in Japan when normal shrimp or prawns won't do, though there is basically no linguistic distinction among the three. Why they are thought to be auspicious is unclear, though one theory points to the bent shape of their back, suggesting old age and longevity. Shrimp are counted *ichio* 一尾, *ippiki* 一匹, and *ippon* 一本.

● 海老で鯛を釣る　　*ebi de tai o tsuru*　"catch a sea bream with a shrimp"

do things the easy way; get a lot of bang for your buck, maximize returns and minimize effort, profit handsomely from a small investment, make a killing; throw a sprat to catch a mackerel

---

○ 「バラの花束なんか持ってどうしたんだい。」
"Bara no hanataba nanka motte dō shita n' dai."
"What're you up to, carrying a bouquet of roses and all?"

「今日は、念願の彼女と初デートなんだ。よくいうだろう『海老 で鯛を釣れ』って。」
"Kyō wa, nengan no kanojo to hatsu dēto nan da. Yoku iu darō 'ebi de tai o tsure' tte."
"Today's my first time out with that chick I've had my eye on, and I'm just trying to make the most of it."

○ 大した努力もしないで、海老で鯛を釣ろうとしてもだめだな。
Taishita doryoku mo shinai de, ebi de tai o tsurō to shite mo dame da na.
Trying to make a killing without making much of an effort just isn't going to work.

🐙 Possibly from the plentifulness of shrimp and their diminutive size compared to sea bream. Used of attempts to spend as little time, money, or effort to attain one's grandiose goals. Also *ebi (de) tai* 海老（で）鯛.

かい（貝）　*kai*　shellfish

☞ *Kai* is the generic term for shellfish of all kinds, univalves and bivalves included. These aquatic animals have been part of the Japanese diet since the earliest times, with kitchen middens containing pottery shards and shell refuse from the Jomon period and beyond, providing researchers with a significant source of information about the lifestyles and diets of early inhabitants of the archipelago.

● 貝のように（口をつぐむ）　　*kai no yō ni (kuchi o tsugumu)*
"(close *one's* mouth) like a clam"

keep *one's* mouth shut, clam up, close up like a clam, button *one's* lip

---

○ 彼は貝のようにその件については口をつぐむばかりだ。

Kare wa kai no yō ni sono ken ni tsuite wa kuchi o tsugumu bakari da.

He clammed up (was closed mouthed) about the incident.

○ 貝のように口を閉ざした男は、その罪を一身に背負って死んでいった。

Kai no yō ni kuchi o tozashita otoko wa, sono tsumi o isshin ni shotte shinde itta.

The man took full responsibility for the crime upon himself and went to the grave without ever breaking his silence.

🐚 From the bivalve's ability to shut down completely, and the difficulty one has in attempting to pry it open once it has closed.

きんぎょ（金魚） *kingyo* goldfish

☞ Perhaps as much a part of teaching human fry responsibility for the care of animals in Japan as in the West, goldfish are said to have been first introduced from China early in the fifteenth century and, typically, improved upon. Since their introduction they have become the most common freshwater fish to take up residence in Japanese homes and to sacrifice their lives in the interest of the larger and more demanding pets that inevitably follow in their tiny wakes (pun intended).

Sold at shrine festivals held throughout Japan during the summer, goldfish are netted by children with small paper nets from troughs at outdoor stalls after paying a small fee to the vendors, only then to be carried home, gasping for life in plastic baggies by proud anglers who have just unwittingly experienced an essential early childhood social indoctrination ritual: to fish in Japan is to stand shoulder to shoulder with dozens of others who have traveled far and paid a fee to those who stock moats, ponds, and rivers with hungry fish. Be that as it may, goldfish are so closely associated with summer that they have even been bestowed with the cultural seal of approval, classification as a "seasonal word" in *renga* and haiku connoting summer.

● 金魚の糞 *kingyo no fun* "goldfish crap"

a tagalong, shadow, hanger-on; *someone* you just can't seem to shake (off)

○ 斉藤君の妹は金魚の糞のように、どこに行くにもお兄さんと一緒だ。

Saitō-kun no imōto wa kingyo no fun no yō ni, doko ni iku ni mo oniisan to issho da.

Saito's little sister is always tagging along after him everywhere he goes.

○ そのバンドのファン達は金魚の糞だ。一日中彼らの後を追いかけ
廻した。

*Sono bando no fan-tachi wa kingyo no fun da. Ichinichi-jū karera
no ato o oikakemawashita.*

A bunch of groupies followed the band around all day.

🐚 A personal favorite of the authors, this colorful metaphoric use will be
readily identified (by anyone who has ever had goldfish) with the difficulty the fish have shaking off their own excrement. Also, but less commonly, *kingyo no unko* 金魚のうんこ.

こい（鯉）　*koi*　carp, koi

☞ We're talking major cultural differences here between the way this
bottom feeder has been traditionally viewed in the East and West. While
it seldom finds its way onto dining tables in the West where it is generally spurned as a garbage fish by anglers who inadvertantly hook it, in
Asia this esteemed denizen of slow-moving rivers, ponds, and lakes, has
long been raised for food or bred for the pleasure its variegated colors
bring sedate viewers. Before modern times in Japan, the *koi* was even
considered superior to the sea bream, or *tai*, and often served as the main
course on auspicious or congratulatory occasions.

The fish's fabled spirit and strength have given rise to the custom of
hanging large carp-shaped wind socks or streamers made of paper or
cloth, one for each male child in a family, on and around Children's Day,
May 5, to celebrate another year of growth and safety.

Carp are counted *ichio* 一尾 or *ippiki* 一匹.

● 鯉の滝登り　*koi no takinobori*　"a carp's climb up a waterfall"

getting ahead; a quick rise to the top (of *one's* profession or
field)

○ 彼の人生はまさに鯉の滝登りであった。

Kare no jinsei wa masa ni koi no takinobori de atta.

His life was a case study of how to get ahead.

○ 最近の若者は鯉の滝登りを夢見る者が少なくなった。

*Saikin no wakamono wa koi no takinobori o yume miru mono ga
sukunaku natta.*

There are fewer and fewer in the younger generation who dream
of making it big in (leaving their mark on) the world.

🐚 According to Chinese legend, the carp alone among all fishes was able
to swim up a waterfall called the Dragon's Gate, *Tōryūmon* 登竜門, on

the upper reaches of the Yellow River, and by so doing was transformed into a dragon itself. In a take-off from this legend, the Japanese idiom *koi no takinobori* has come to express a quick rise to the top of one's profession, or getting ahead. See next entry.

● 登竜門   *Tōryūmon*   "climb the Dragon's Gate"
pass muster, get over an important hurdle

○ この文学賞は若手作家の登竜門と呼ばれている。
Kono bungaku-shō wa wakate-sakka no Tōryūmon to yobarete iru.
This literary prize is considered to guarantee (be the gateway to) success as an author.

○ 君にとってこのプロジェクトは重役への登竜門だ。
Kimi ni totte kono purojekuto wa jūyaku e no Tōryūmon da.
Success (or failure) on this project will seal your fate as a future director with the company.

♨ See note under preceding entry, *koi no takinobori* 鯉の滝登り, for explanation.

● まな板の鯉   *manaita no koi*   "a carp on the cutting board"
be resigned to one's fate, be ready to take one's punishment

○ いよいよ明日は試験ですね。勉強しなくていいの。
Iyoiyo ashita wa shiken desu ne. Benkyō shinakute ii no.
The test's tomorrow, isn't it? Hadn't you better be hitting the books?

○ まな板の鯉の心境だよ。
Manaita no koi no shinkyō da yo.
It's out'a my hands now. I'll just have to take what's comin' to me.

○ 裁判官の前に立ったときはまさにまな板の鯉になった。
Saiban-kan no mae ni tatta toki wa masa ni manaita no koi ni natta.
Standing there in front of the judge, I felt like I was just waiting for the axe to fall.

♨ Of a situation over which one has no control and the likely unpleasant outcome, which one has no choice but to accept. From anthropomorphizing of a carp's imagined emotional state as it lies on the chef's cutting board awaiting beheading, disembowelment, and drawing and quartering in the service of culinary pleasure.

ごり （鮴） *gori* goby

☞ These small freshwater, spiny-finned fishes are known to school and swim upstream dozens of kilometers to visit relatives during the summer holidays. Apparently it's the only time of year they can get away from work around the estuaries, where they usually attach themselves to rocks by way of a unique ventral suction disk formed by their pelvic fins, which are joined together.

Gobi are counted *ichibe* 一尾 or *ippiki* 一匹.

● ごり押し　*gorioshi*　"goby push"
ram (push) through; steamroll, bulldoze

○ そういうごり押しをするからおまえはみんなから嫌われるんだ。

Sō iu gorioshi o suru kara omae wa minna kara kirawareru n' da.

That's why nobody wants to have anything to do with you, 'cause you're always ramming stuff down their throats.

○ あの代議士ごり押しして急行を自分の駅に臨時停車させて問題になった。

Ano daigi-shi gorioshi shite kyūkō o jibun no eki ni rinji-teisha sasete mondai ni natta.

He's the representative that caused all the fuss when he forced an express train to make an unscheduled stop at his station.

○ それはごり押しですよ。あの成績では、息子さんを入学させるわけにはいきません。

Sore wa gorioshi desu yo. Ano seiseki de wa, musuko-san o nyūgaku saseru wake ni wa ikimasen.

You are asking far too much. There is no way your son can be accepted at the school with those grades.

✄ From the tremendous efforts expended by these tiny fish to swim long distances upstream to spawn.

さば （鯖） *saba* mackerel

☞ This common saltwater fish has long been caught and eaten in great numbers in Japan, and is becoming increasingly prized in the autumn for its oily flesh, now that other species have been overfished throughout the world.

The mackerel is also known in Japan for the speed with which it rots from within while remaining apparently fresh on the outside. This is due to the presence of histidine, a crystalline basic amino acid, in its flesh.

After the fish's death, the histidine is rapidly transformed into histimine, which can cause allergic rashes.

Mackerel are counted *ichio* 一尾 or *ippiki* 一匹 when alive or uncleaned, and *ichimai* 一枚 when they have been filleted or butterflied.

● さばを読む　*saba o yomu*　"read mackerel"
fudge, miscount, cheat on (fudge) the count

○ パーティーの参加人数を幹事がさばを読んで、儲けたらしいぞ。
Pāti no sanka-ninzū o kanji ga saba o yonde, mōketa rashii zo.
It looks like the guy who was in charge of the party padded the number of people coming and pocketed the difference (between that number and the amount received from his office for the party based on his padded figures).

○ 24歳だって、ちょっとさば読んでるんじゃないの、あの人。
Nijū-yon-sai datte, chotto saba yonde 'ru n' ja nai no, ano hito.
Says she's 24? I'll bet she's fudging it a little bit.

 🦐 Sources differ slightly on the origin of this idiom, but seem to agree that the practice of counting mackerel (some say by twos because so many of them are caught at one time) very fast at fish markets is done intentionally in hopes of adding to or subtracting from the actual number, whichever is in the counter's favor. The *"o"* is often dropped, especially in spoken Japanese. Also *saba yomi* 鯖読み.

さめ（鮫）　*same*　shark

☞ You'd think that with a hundred or so species in the oceans around Japan and the Japanese dependence upon the seas for food that there would have been sufficient contact over the centuries with these killers to produce a few idioms about agressiveness or bloodthirstyness, but no, this fish is oddly missing from the lexicon. Basically all that can be said about its importance, linguistic or otherwise, is that its flesh is an important ingredient in fish paste, or *kamaboko*.

● 鮫肌　*samehada*　"sharkskin"
rough skin

○ 彼女可愛いんだけど、鮫肌だよね。
Kanojo kawaii n' da kedo, samehada da yo ne.
She's cute all right, but her skin's like sandpaper.

○ この生地は一見滑らかそうに見えるが触ってみるとちょうど鮫肌
のようです。

Kono kiji wa ikken namerakasō ni mieru ga sawatte miru to chōdo samehada no yō desu.

At first glance this material appears to be smooth, but feel it for yourself and you'll see how rough it is.

✌ Dictionaries indicate usage limited to descriptions of human skin, but experience reveals that its appearance with *no yō da* indicates a broader sense. No relation to the fabric by the same name in English long associated with fashion criminals.

たい （鯛） *tai* sea bream / red snapper

☞ Why is snapper served as the main course on many joyous occasions in Japan? The kanji for *tai* is written with two components, the fish radical and the element for vicinity, suggesting that the fish has long been plentiful in the seas surrounding the archipelago. This inference is supported by the mention of the fish in Japan's oldest extant poetry compendium, the *Man'yoshū,* which is thought to have been compiled around the end of the Nara period (710–784). Having said that, the more immediate reason seems to be a simple play on words, since the Japanese for happy or joyous is *medetai,* leading one to speculate that either some ancient wag or person with a vested interest in the sale of the fish contrived a linguistic inducement to its consumption.

● 腐っても鯛　*kusatte mo tai*　"a rotten sea bream is still a sea bream"

once a winner, always a winner; an old eagle is better than a young crow; a diamond on a dunghill is still a diamond

---

○「なんだベンツ買ったって、中古じゃないか。」
"Nan da bentsu katta tte, chūko ja nai ka."
"Thought you said you bought a Mercedes? But what's this, man, a used one?"

「腐っても鯛というじゃないか。」
"Kusatte mo tai to iu ja nai ka."
"Hey, it's still a Mercedes."

○ 腐っても鯛、この桐のタンスは20年以上も使っているが少しもきしみがない。
Kusatte mo tai, kono kiri no tansu wa nijū-nen ijō mo tsukatte iru ga sukoshi mo kishimi ga nai.
There's no denying quality. Had this paulownia chest of drawers for over twenty years, and it's as solid as ever.

ꝸ From the notion that something superior remains so even in old age. The idiom arises from the fact that the flesh of the snapper is relatively fat-free, and the taste, therefore, does not decline significantly when not perfectly fresh.

たこ（蛸）　*tako*　octopus

☞　Although this mollusk dwells at the bottom of the sea, it surfaces regularly in the lexicon through a broad variety of idioms and expressions that draw from such things as the unique octopodous configuration of its arms (legs, really) and the reversal of the relative position of body parts, with the trunk sitting atop the head to which the legs appear to be directly attached. There is even a financial term, *tako-haitō* 蛸配当, describing a bogus dividend paid from a corporation's assets to investors even though the bottom line fails to show a profit. This derives from the superstitious belief that starvation drives the octopus to the ultimately suicidal practice of devouring its own legs in order to survive. The earthenware jar used to catch octopi, *takotsubo* 蛸壷, has lent its name to the Japanese military's equivalent of our "foxhole," a shallow one or two-man trench dug to protect soldiers from enemy fire.

Unlike in the West, where its demonization has led to it being called a "devilfish," with one American naturalist, Frank Norris, even entitling his great novel depicting the Southern Pacific Railroad and its far-reaching control of California wheat farmers, *The Octopus*; and notwithstanding recent slang coinages, such as the first entry below indicating that its image is not one of uniform popularity, this cephalopod is generally held in Japan to be friendly toward man and is often depicted as intelligent and mischievous.

Octopi are counted *ippiki* 一匹 and, less commonly, *ippai* 一杯 (because of the shape of the pot, perhaps), unless they are gutted, flattened, and hung out to dry, when they are counted *ichiren* 一連.

● タコ　*tako*　"octopus"
birdbrain, bunhead, dope, dummy, fool, idiot, imbecile, ninny, stupid

---

○ あっ！映画のチケット忘れたじゃないか、このタコ。
A! Eiga no chiketto wasureta ja nai ka, kono tako.
Duh, you didn't forget to bring the tickets for the movie, did you, numbnuts?

○「タコ！」
"Tako!"
"Boy am I dumb! / Fuck me!"

「どうしたの。」
"Dōshita no."
"What's wrong?"

「財布落とした。」
"Saifu otoshita."
"Oh, I lost my wallet somewhere."

✌ As exemplified above, this recent addition to the language of youth can be used of others or the speaker, and may become the modern equivalent of the more common *baka.*

● たこ入道　*tako-nyūdō*　"a tonsured octopus"
a bald person, baldy, cue ball, egghead, skin head

○ 山田先生は生徒の間でたこ入道と呼ばれている。
Yamada-sensei wa seito no aida de tako-nyūdō to yobarete iru.
His students call Mr. Yamada "cue ball."

○ あのたこ入道みたいな俳優なんていったけ？
Ano tako-nyūdō mitai na haiyū nante itta ke?
What was that bald actor's name?

✌ Jocular reference to a bald person. From the resemblance of the octopus's trunk, which sits where its head *should* be, to a bald pate.

● たこ部屋　*tako-beya*　"an octopus room"
a pigsty, pit, dump

○ 不法入国した労働者はたこ部屋のようなところに押し込められていた。
Fuhō-nyūkoku shita rōdō-sha wa tako-beya no yō na tokoro ni oshikomerarete ita.
Illegal immigrant laborers were herded into disgusting labor camps like so many cattle.

○ その旅館の部屋はまるでたこ部屋のようで、雑魚寝する貧乏旅行者でいっぱいだった。
Sono ryokan no heya wa maru de tako-beya no yō de, zako-ne suru binbō-ryokō-sha de ippai datta.
The inn was a veritable pigsty, with down-at-the-heel travelers sprawled all over the floor.

✌ From their resemblance to the masonry jars used to catch octopuses and the difficulty the animal has escaping once it has entered, this term was originally used of the forced labor camps at the mines of Hokkaido prior to World War II, where squalid living conditions prevailed and from which escape was all but impossible.

↪ *butagoya* 豚小屋

● たこ足配線　*takoashi-haisen*　"electrical cords (like) octopus legs"
an overloaded electrical outlet; a scramble of electrical cords

---

○ こんなたこ足配線してたら、火事になるよ。
Konna takoashi-haisen shite 'tara, kaji ni naru yo.
You're going to cause a fire by overloading an outlet like this.

○ 彼の部屋はたこ足配線で足の踏み場に困った。
Kare no heya wa takoashi-haisen de ashi no fumiba ni komatta.
His room was so cluttered with electrical cords running here and there that you could hardly find a place to stand.

⚒ From the resemblance of the many cords trailing out from an overloaded electrical outlet to the eight legs of the octopus.

┌─────────────────────────────────────┐
│　どじょう（泥鰌）　*dojō* loach │
└─────────────────────────────────────┘

☞　Unfamiliar to most Westerners, these small freshwater fish, variously said to be related to minnows or carps, are common in streams, marshes, and rice paddies throughout Japan. They are eaten in a variety of ways, including as a tabletop casserole dish called *yanagawa* 柳川, in which the little critters are boiled alive with eggs. Their futile attempts to escape the increasing heat drives them headlong into a radiating pattern away from the center of the pot, creating a delightful artistic, if not culinary, motif for the enjoyment of cold-blooded diners. Many Tokyo restaurants specializing in loach dishes advertise their menu by corrupting the four-phonetic character name *dojō* どじょう as *dozeu* どぜう. By deleting a phonetic character they avoid a word composed of four letters, the Japanese word for four, *shi*, being homonymous with that for death. Anything in fours is considered inauspicious.

● どじょうひげ　*dojō hige*　"a loach mustache"
a thin (sparse) mustache

○ あのどじょうひげのお爺さん知ってる？
Ano dojō hige no ojiisan shitte 'ru?
You know that old guy with the skinny little mustache?

○ 考え事をするときどじょうひげを引っ張るのが父の癖だった。

Kangaegoto o suru toki dojō hige o hipparu no ga chichi no kuse datta.

My dad always used to tug at his thin mustache when he was thinking about something.

🐇 From the resemblance of such a mustache to the ten barbels growing around the mouth of a loach.

● 柳の下にいつもどじょうはいない *yanagi no shita ni itsumo dojō wa inai* "there is not always a loach under the willow"

there is a limit to luck (from the tale of a man who once caught a loach under a certain willow tree but was never able to repeat the feat)

○ 去年のダービーでは大穴を当てたが、柳の下にいつもどじょうは いないということか。

Kyonen no dābī de wa ōana o ateta ga, yanagi no shita ni itsumo dojō wa inai to iu koto ka.

Last year I made a killing on a sleeper in the derby, but no such luck this year.

○ 前の試験はたまたまヤマが当たっただけでしょう。柳の下にどじ ょうは二匹いないよ。

Mae no shiken wa tamatama yama ga atatta dake deshō. Yanagi no shita ni dojō wa nihiki inai yo.

I just lucked out on the last test. No way it'll ever happen again.

とど（鯔） *todo* (a grown) mullet

☞ A common food fish found throughout the warm waters of the world, the mullet lends its name, at least one of its names, to a single idiom.

● とどのつまり *todo no tsumari* "the end mullet"

in the end, finally, eventually; when all is said and done, in the final analysis

---

○ とどのつまり、彼は女にだまされたということだよ。

Todo no tsumari, kare wa onna ni damasareta to iu koto da yo.

He ended up getting taken in by some woman.

○ とどのつまり、マスコミが騒いだだけに終わった。

Todo no tsumari, masukomi ga sawaida dake ni owatta.

When all was said and done, it was nothing but media hype.

🐟 This idiom comes from the fact that this fish goes through so many name changes as it grows that it must suffer an identity crisis. Called *oboko, subashiri, ina, bora*, and the final one from which this idiom is derived, *todo*; hence the meaning "eventually" or "finally."

5

昆虫類
INSECTS / BUGS

Recent scientific data indicate that creepy crawly things like insects and spiders make up some 99 percent of all species on earth. According to Natalie Angier, a New York Times Service writer, that amounts to somewhere in the neighborhood of 300 pounds of them for every pound of us! And these astronomical figures remain undented, despite the best efforts of myriads of junior entomologists to even the odds by scouring the neighborhoods, insect nets and boxes in hand, searching for something to pull the legs off of. The large variety of species, their proximity to humans, as well as their peculiar characteristics and behavior all contribute to the large number of expressions deriving from bugs. There are, for example, "centipede races" 百足競争 *mukade kyōsō* at school track meets, in which a dozen or so competitors are joined in a line at the ankles by ropes and get all tangled up, running a predetermined distance, as well as "rice-pounding" locusts, コメツキバッタ *kometsuki-batta*, referring to locusts that move up and down as if pounding rice when held up by the hind legs. From this unusual behavior and the observation that Japanese toadies are always bowing and scraping, comes the metaphoric use of this term to refer to a sycophant, apple-polisher, or ass-licker.

虻 *abu* a horsefly

☞ Anyone who has been bitten by one knows a little of what horses

123

and cattle must go through and at least one reason they have long tails. The females of this species are bloodsuckers. They'll take a piece out of your hide if you give 'em a chance.

Abu are counted *ippiki* 一匹.

● 虻蜂取らず　*abuhachi torazu*　"catch neither the horsefly nor the bee"

try to do two things and fail at both; fall between two stools

---

○ そんなに欲張っても虻蜂取らずになったら元も子もないよ。

Sonna ni yokubatte mo abuhachi torazu ni nattara moto mo ko mo nai yo.

Let your greed get the better of you and you'll end up falling flat on your face.

○ 彼はいろいろな事業に手を出しすぎて、結局虻蜂取らずとなった。

Kare wa iroiro na jigyō ni te o dashisugite, kekkyoku abuhachi torazu to natta.

He overextended by branching out into all kinds of businesses and went bust.

✌ There are several variations of this expression: *abu mo hachi mo torazu* 虻も蜂も取らず, *abu mo torazu hachi mo torazu* 虻も取らず蜂も取らず, and *abu mo torazu hachi ni sasareru* 虻も取らず蜂に刺される. The first two are reconfigurations of the idiom as it appears in the entry; the third translates literally as "not only fail to catch the horsefly, but get stung by a bee (in the process)." A similar expression is *nito o ou mono wa itto o (mo) ezu* 二兎を追う者は一兎を（も）得ず, precisely the same as (and perhaps derived from) the English "If you run after two hares, you will catch neither." It is effectively the opposite of *isseki-nicho* 一石二鳥, or "(killing) two birds with one stone."

蟻　*ari*　ant

☞ Fact: the total body weight of all the ants on the face of the earth is approximately the same as that of all its human inhabitants. Ants appear often in folk tales, owing to their social behavior and other fanciful similarities to humankind. Any unusal activity by ants is also thought to presage events. For example, when ants are observed fighting it is believed to warn of impending rain.

Ants are counted *ippiki* 一匹 or *ichiwa* 一羽. While you might imagine that the latter is used exclusively of the winged varieties, you would be wrong, but don't ask why.

● 蟻地獄　*ari-jigoku*　"a doodlebug"
quicksand, a trap

○ 借金の蟻地獄にはまった彼はとうとう会社の金に手を出した。
Shakkin no ari-jigoku ni hamatta kare wa tōtō kaisha no kane ni te o dashita.
Having fallen deeply in debt, he ended up dipping into corporate funds.

○ 彼は新興宗教にうっかり引っかかり、蟻地獄に落ちる思いであった。
Kare wa shinkō-shūkyō ni ukkari hikkakari, ari-jigoku ni ochiru omoi de atta.
After falling in with some new religion, he began to feel trapped.

○ 蟻地獄のような売春組織にひっかかった彼女はその後行方がわからなくなった。
Ari-jikoku no yō na baishun-soshiki ni hikkakatta kanojo wa sono ato yukue ga wakaranaku natta.
She was never heard from again once she had been sucked into the quicksand of organized prostitution.

🐛 The doodlebug, for those uninitiated into the lexicon of bugology, is the larva of the ant lion. This energy-efficient little bugger lies in ambush at the bottom of a conical sand trap for duffers (and ants) that slide down that slippery slope into its arthropodan mandibles. Despite parallels with Kobo Abe's *Woman in the Dunes,* there is no evidence that the female of the species is particularly rapacious. As for the idiom, it derives from the trap its namesake constructs, and is used of a condition into which one has fallen and from which escape is all but impossible. Perhaps taking a hint from entomology, enterprising city planners in Japan have devised an ingenious concrete contraption (much to the delight of harried mothers) that resembles the doodlebug's lair, only maybe 500,000 times bigger and without the jaws of death lurking at the bottom. Placed strategically in city parks, these *ari-jigoku* effectively restrict a child's wanderings, freeing the mother for a few moments of peace and prattle.

● 蟻の一穴　*ari no ikketsu*　"an ant hole"
a tiny mistake can lead to disaster

○ 蟻の一穴とならないよう、もう一度チェックしよう。
Ari no ikketsu to naranai yō, mō ichido chekku shiyō.
I'm going to look this over again to make sure there's nothing in here that could be my undoing.

o 作業員の不注意が蟻の一穴となり、その現場は一瞬にしてがれき
の山となった。

Sagyō-in no fu-chūi ga ari no ikketsu to nari, sono genba wa is-shun ni shite gareki no yama to natta.

A simple slip-up by one of the workers turned the construction site into a mountain of rubble in an instant.

🦋 From an ancient parable about a 10,000-foot dike that collapsed due to a single tunnel dug by an ant, this idiom is often used as an admonition against oversight or omission.

● 蟻の這いでる隙もない *ari no haideru suki mo nai* "without space for so much as an ant to crawl out"
completely surrounded, sealed off, cordoned off

---

o 強盗が立てこもった民家の周りには蟻の這いでる隙もないほどの
警官が包囲した。

Gōtō ga tatekomotta minka no mawari ni wa ari no haideru suki mo nai hodo no keikan ga hōi shita.

The house where the robber was holed up was sealed off water-tight by the police. / Nobody could possibly get through the police cordon around the house where the robber was hiding out.

o 国連の平和維持部隊は包囲され蟻の這いでる隙もなかった。

Kokuren no heiwaiji-butai wa hōi sare ari no haideru suki mo nakatta.

United Nations peacekeepers were completely sealed off from the outside.

🦋 Used most commonly of, or by, law enforcement or the military.

| おけら（螻蛄） *okera* mole cricket |

☞ Built for digging, this inch-long subterranean can sometimes be found under stones or down wood. In the fall its cry—*jī* ジー—is commonly said to be the cry of earthworms. Mole crickets are counted *ippiki* 一匹.

● おけら（螻蛄） *okera* (or *kera*) "a mole cricket"
be (flat) broke, cleaned out, penniless, tapped (out), wiped out

---

o 彼女は競馬にボーナス全部つぎ込んで結局おけらになった。

Kanojo wa keiba ni bōnasu zenbu tsugikonde kekkyoku okera ni natta.

She blew her whole bonus on the ponies and now she's flat-ass broke.

○ おけらだと言っていた彼がどうやって海外旅行なんか行けたのだろう？

Okera da to itte ita kare ga dō yatte kaigai-ryokō nanka iketa no darō?

How'd that dude ever afford to travel abroad when he was just saying he was tapped out and all?

🐚 Idiomatic use apparently derives from the association of the Japanese body language for being broke, both arms extended over one's head as in a "banzai" gesture, with the appearance of the mole cricket. Whoever said the Japanese weren't creative? Originally gamblers' and pickpockets' argot, it is usually written in katakana.

蚊 *ka* mosquito

☞ With around a hundred species of this diminutive pest indigenous to Japan, it is not surprising to discover that it figures in a number of common idioms, none of which are particularly flattering. The mosquito is said to have metamorphosed from the dead body of an ogre, whose curse upon humanity the female of the family, with its elongated proboscis, is banefully adapted to carry out. It wasn't too long ago that Japanese spread their futons out under mosquito nets during the summer for protection from the pesky bloodsuckers. Idioms that incorporate the insect are generally of delicate or otherwise insubstantial things. The sound associated with the mosquito is *būn* ブーン. It is counted *ippiki* 一匹.

● 蚊トンボ *ka-tonbo* "a mosquito dragonfly"
a crane fly; a skinny person; a rail, a rattlebones, skinny-bones; (of a tall person) a beanstalk, beanpole

○ 鈴木さんは蚊トンボのような人。
Suzuki-san wa ka-tonbo no yō na hito.
Suzuki's a regular beanpole.

○「どんなのがタイプ？」
"Donna no ga taipu?"
"What kind'a guys do you like?"

「蚊トンボは嫌ね。」
"Ka-tonbo wa iya ne."

"No skinnybones for me."

🐛 Of a tall, thin person, often used jocularly. While the long-legged crane fly resembles a large mosquito, it is not one. Nor does it bite. This idiom is included here for convenience only.

● 蚊に刺されたほどにも思わぬ　*ka ni sasareta hodo ni mo omowanu* "consider *something* to be less than a mosquito bite"
(of the person) don't care a bit, could(n't) care less; (of the inconvenience) a fleabite

---

○ あいつ先生に怒られても、蚊に刺されたほどにも思ってないよ。
Aitsu sensei ni okorarete mo, ka ni sasareta hodo ni mo omotte 'nai yo.
He doesn't give a shit if the teacher gets mad at him. / It doesn't mean diddly squat to him if the teacher goes ballistic.

○ あの人は相当な資産家だから、今回の株下落も蚊に刺されたほどに思っていない様子だったよ。
Ano hito wa sōtō na shisan-ka da kara, konkai no kabu-geraku mo ka ni sasareta hodo ni omotte inai yōsu datta yo.
He's pretty well off so it doesn't look like the recent decline in the stock market is any big deal to him.

○ たいていの大企業にとって住民からの訴訟は蚊に刺されたほどに思わぬものだ。
Taitei no dai-kigyō ni totte jūmin kara no soshō wa ka ni sasareta hodo ni omowanu mono da.
A law suit by some citizen is about as troublesome to most big businesses as a fleabite.

🐛 The idiom is always negative, reflecting the view that there is no influence or change as a result of the action to which it refers.

● 蚊の鳴くような声　*ka no naku yō na koe* "a cry like a mosquito's"
a faint (barely audible, thin) voice, a whisper

○ そんな蚊の鳴くような声では面接に落ちてしまうよ。
Sonna ka no naku yō na koe de wa mensetsu ni ochite shimau yo.
You'll never make it beyond the interview if you mumble like that.

○ 彼は蚊の鳴くような声で先生の質問に答えた。

Kare wa ka no naku yō na koe de sensei no shitsumon ni kotaeta.

He answered the teacher's question in a barely audible voice.

🦋 From the all but inaudible sound made by the wings of the dipterous pest. Often used of a timid person or one who lacks self-confidence.

● 蚊の涙 *ka no namida* "a mosquito's tear"

(of an amount of money) very little, next to nothing

○ 今年の昇給は蚊の涙だ。

Kotoshi no shōkyū wa ka no namida da.

The raise I got this year didn't amount to much. / I didn't get shit for a raise this year.

○ そんな蚊の涙ほどの報酬では、人は集まらない。

Sonna ka no namida hodo no hōshū de wa, hito wa atsumaranai.

You're not going to get many job applicants by offering a pittance like that.

↪ *suzume no namida* 雀の涙

蜘蛛 *kumo* spider

☞   The species of these largely misunderstood arthropods found in Japan are despised there just there as they are elsewhere, though the shrieks and cries of Japanese arachnophobes seem somehow shriller. Bad boys of the insect kingdom, spiders fare poorly in folk wisdom, which dictates that nocturnal spiders are to be killed while diurnal spiders are spared. "Dirt Spider," or *tsuchigumo* 土蜘蛛 was a derogatory appelation given to a legendary race who refused to be subjugated by the early rulers of the Yamato court.

Some households in Japan still believe that a spider wrapped in tissue paper and placed in a closet will guarantee financial good fortune. Were it only so easy.

Spiders are counted *ippiki* 一匹.

● 蜘蛛の子を散らす *kumo no ko o chirasu* "scatter baby spiders"

scatter out, disperse

○ 群衆は機動隊の催涙弾を受け蜘蛛の子を散らすように逃げた。

Gunshū wa kidō-tai no sairuidan o uke kumo no ko o chirasu yō ni nigeta.

The crowd lit out in all directions when the riot police lobbed in
teargas.

○ デモ隊は戦車の現れるのを見て蜘蛛の子を散らすように逃げた。
*Demo-tai wa sensha no arawareru no o mite kumo no ko o chirasu
yō ni nigeta.*
Demonstrators took to their heels and scattered in all directions at
the sight of the tanks moving in.

○ 少年達はガラスの割れる音を聞いて蜘蛛の子を散らすように逃げた。
*Shōnen-tachi wa garasu no wareru oto o kiite kumo no ko o chi-
rasu yō ni nigeta.*
The boys were all assholes and elbows when they heard the glass
breaking.

🖋 Used often, though not exclusively, with *yō ni nigeru*. From the observation that baby spiders rush out in all directions when a sack full of
them is ripped open.

げじげじ（蚰蜒） *gejigeji* house centipede

☞ Just why this and other caterpillar-like critters are so despicable is
unclear. One suggestion is that they have fifteen pairs of legs, not the
fifty it would take to make them full-fledged centipedes. They are
counted *ippiki* 一匹.

● げじげじ（蚰蜒） *gejigeji* house centipede
a creep, jerk, rat, skunk, bastard

○ あのげじげじやろうめ。
Ano gejigeji yarō me!
That creepy son of a bitch!

○ 僕は小さい頃げじげじと呼ばれていた。
Boku wa chiisai koro gejigeji to yobarete ita.
They used to call me "creep" when I was little.

🖋 Of a strongly disliked person. Used most commonly by children.

↪ *kemushi* 毛虫

● げじげじ眉毛 *gejigeji-mayuge* "millipede eyebrows"
bushy (thick and shaggy) eyebrows

○ あのげじげじ眉毛のお爺さん相当な資産家らしいよ。

Ano gejigeji-mayuge no ojiisan sōtō na shisan-ka rashii yo.

That old guy with the bushy eyebrows is supposed to be filthy rich.

○ 細川さんとこの男の人達はお爺さんから孫までみんなげじげじ眉毛だね。

Hosokawa-san toko no otoko no hitotachi wa ojiisan kara mago made minna gejigeji-mayuge da ne.

All the men in the Hosokawa clan, from grandfather to grandson, have thick, shaggy eyebrows.

☙ From the resemblance of such eyebrows to caterpillars. Can be pejorative. Seldom used of women.

毛虫 *kemushi* caterpillar

☞ Everything that's true of centipedes is true of caterpillars, except for the number of legs they have.

● 毛虫 *kemushi* "hairy bug"
a creep, crud, jerk, rat, skunk, bastard

○ あのタレント、小さい頃はこの近所では毛虫と呼ばれてたんだよ。

Ano tarento, chiisai koro wa kono kinjo de wa kemushi to yobarete 'ta n' da yo.

That celebrity used to be known as a creep around this neighborhood when he was little.

○ 昔はよくおとなしい子を「弱虫毛虫はさんで捨てろ！」と言ってからかったことがあるよ。

Mukashi wa yoku otonashii ko o "yowamushi kemushi hasande sutero!" to itte karakatta koto ga aru yo.

Way back when, I used to tease quieter kids, saying "Cry baby, cry baby, nobody likes a cry baby!"

☙ Used by children pejoratively to describe a strongly disliked person.

☙ *gejigeji* げじげじ（蚰蜒）

虱 *shirami* louse

☞ Like other diminutive blood-sucking parasites, lice generally figure in unflattering expressions and maxims. Their tiny size also lends itself to comments regarding minutiae. Lice are counted *ippiki* 一匹, and move around so quickly that the same one is often counted more than once.

● 虱つぶし（に）　*shirami tsubushi (ni)*　"lice crushing"
comb (a place for), search (go through/over) with a fine-tooth
comb; check out every lead one by one

○ 部屋中虱つぶしに捜したが、結局その書類は見つからなかった。
*Heya-jū shirami tsubushi ni sagashita ga, kekkyoku sono shorui
wa mitsukaranakatta.*
I went through the house with a fine-tooth comb but couldn't lo-
cate the papers.

○ 警察は犯人の手がかりがないかどうか犯行現場一帯を虱つぶしに
した。
*Keisatsu wa hannin no tegakari ga nai ka dō ka, hankō-genba ittai
o shirami tsubushi ni shita.*
In hopes of finding clues that would help identify the perpetrator,
police investigators conducted a thorough search of the crime
scene.

✌ The word *shirami* is often written in katakana, presumably because
the kanji is difficult to read and not included in the government's *Jōyō
Kanji* list. It almost always appears in the form *o shirami tsubushi ni
suru,* where the verb has to do with searching or investigation possibili-
ties. It derives from the image of someone crushing lice one by one,
hence being very thorough. Unfortunately, "nitpick" is a false friend, for
the Japanese lacks any sense of niggling or criticism, which is inherent in
the English.

だに（壁蝨）　*dani*　tick

☞ This eight-legged parasite is related to spiders but liked a lot less,
wherever it is found. Urban infestations of the hearty bloodsuckers have
caused apartment dwellers headaches—and a lot of itching and scratching—in recent years. Ticks are counted *ippiki* 一匹.

● だに　*dani*　tick
a hood, gangster, punk; a good-for-nothing, parasite, scumbag

○ あいつはこの町のだにだから、早くいなくなればいいんだ。
*Aitsu wa kono machi no dani da kara, hayaku inaku nareba ii n'
da.*
He's like a plague on the town. The sooner he's out'a here the
better.

○ あんなだにのような奴、ろくな死に方しないよ。

Anna dani no yō na yatsu, roku na shinikata shinai yo.

A punk like that's gonna end up face down in some alley.

🦋 By extension from the fact that ticks are parasites sucking the lifeblood of others, this expression is usually used of those involved in underworld activities or the likes.

玉虫　*tamamushi*　jewel beetle

☞ This iridescent beetle's greenish wings and reddish gold striped body reflect light beautifully. It has given its name to a type of weaving, *tamamushi-ori,* that incorporates threads of different colors in the warp and woof so as to reflect light in a rainbow of colors, depending upon the angle from which it is viewed. Jewel beetles are counted *ippiki* 一匹

● 玉虫色　*tamamushi-iro*　"jewel-beetle colored"
ambiguous, equivocal, obscure, enigmatic, weasel-worded; open for interpretation; clear as mud

---

○ 今度の調停案はまさに玉虫色だ。

Kondo no chōtei-an wa masa ni tamamushi-iro da.

The compromise proposal is about as clear as mud. / It's anybody's guess what the compromise plan actually means.

○ 会長の説明はまったく玉虫色で会社が潰れる恐れもあるぞ。

Kaichō no setsumei wa mattaku tamamushi-iro de kaisha ga tsubureru osore mo aru zo.

The chairperson's explanation was so weasel-worded that I wouldn't be surprised to see the company go belly up.

○ 記者会見での代表の見解は玉虫色の表現ばかりであった。

Kisha-kaiken de no daihyō no kenkai wa tamamushi-iro no hyōgen bakari de atta.

The explanation offered by the rep at the press conference was just a lot of smoke and mirrors.

🦋 Of decisions, explanations, wording, and the like that can be interpreted in various ways depending on how they are viewed.

蝶　*chō*　butterfly

☞ A symbol of beauty, there are over 250 known varieties of this diurnal four-winged insect in Japan. Unlike their poor sisters, the moths, butterflies rest with their wings folded vertically and show no monomaniacal or suicidal tendencies when exposed to light. Also called *chōchō* or *chōcho* 蝶蝶, their flight is expressed onomatopoeically in Japanese as *hirahira to tobu* ヒラヒラと飛ぶ, or fluttering. They are counted in various ways: *ichiwa* 一羽, *ippiki* 一匹, or *ittō* 一頭, the last usually reserved for counting large mammals.

● 蝶よ花よ　*chō yo hana yo*　"O butterfly, O flower"
　shower affection on one's darling daughter (son), bring up
　one's daughter (son) like a princess (prince)

○ 蝶よ花よと育てられた彼女はわがままばかり言っている。
　Chō yo hana yo to sodaterareta kanojo wa wagamama bakari itte iru.
　Pampered all her life, she's always got to have her own way.

○ 長い間子宝に恵まれなかったその夫婦は一粒種の娘を蝶よ花よと
　育てた。
　Nagai aida kodakara ni megumarenakatta sono fūfu wa hitotsubu-dane no musume o chō yo hana yo to sodateta.
　Childless for many years, the doting couple brought up their dar-
　ling daughter like a princess.

⚑ Similar to *neko kawaigari* 猫かわいがり, in the sense of showering affection on someone, *chō yo hana yo* differs in that it is used specifically
about bringing up one's own child, almost always a daughter. Accord-
ingly, it appears almost exclusively with the verb *sodatsu* 育つ.

┌───┐
とんぼ（蜻蛉）　*tonbo*　dragonfly
└───┘

☞　These delightful creatures formerly numbered in the zillions in
Japan, where around two hundred species have been identified. Although
numbers have decreased with urbanization, they remain a national favorite. Early texts recounting the mythological creation of the Japanese
archipelago refer to the largest island with a word now thought by schol-
ars to mean dragonfly. They were also formerly regarded as the embodied spirit of the rice plant (and harbinger of abundant harvests) or, in
some regions, as the god of the paddy fields. The red dragonfly in particular was regarded as transporter of the spirits of departed souls. Children
are especially discouraged from pulling off the wings of this insect.
Dragonflies are counted *ippiki* 一匹.

● 尻切れとんぼ　*shirikire-tonbo*　"a dragonfly with its tail
　broken off"
　unfinished, half-finished, half-done; fizzle out, sputter; start

with a bang and end with a whimper; (of negotiations or discussions) be abruptly broken off

---

○ おまえの話はいつも尻切れとんぼだ。

Omae no hanashi wa itsumo shirikire-tonbo da .

You never finish what you start out to say.

○ 交渉は2時間以上も続いたにもかかわらず尻切れとんぼに終わった。

Kōshō wa niji-kan ijō mo tsuzuita ni mo kakawarazu shirikire-tonbo ni owatta.

Negotiations continued for more than two hours before being broken off.

● とんぼ返り　*tonbogaeri*　"a dragonfly turnaround"
1. (in acrobatics) a midair somersault; (in swimming) a somersault turn

---

○ 彼はとんぼ返りが得意な役者だ。

Kare wa tonbogaeri ga tokui na yakusha da.

That actor's good at doing midair somersaults.

○ さあ今日はクロールととんぼ返りを練習しましょう。

Sā kyō wa kurōru to tonbogaeri o renshū shimashō.

OK, today we're going to practice the crawl and somersault turns.

---

2. (of a journey) a quick return (without a layover)

○ 今日は東京と札幌のとんぼ返りの出張だった。

Kyō wa Tokyo to Sapporo no tonbogaeri no shutchō datta.

I had to go from Tokyo to Sapporo and back on business today.

○ 香港に到着したとたん会社からの連絡で、休む暇もなくとんぼ返りさせられた。

Honkon ni tōchaku shita totan kaisha kara no renraku de, yasumu hima mo naku tonbogaeri saserareta.

No sooner had I arrived in Hong Kong than a message from the office had me turning around to head back without a moment's rest.

🐝 Of a quick trip from one place to another in which little time is spent at the destination, and the return is to the point of origin. From the dragonfly's ability to change direction quickly in flight.

● とんぼ眼鏡　*tonbo-megane*　"dragonfly eyeglasses"
big, round glasses (sunglasses)

○ これ若い頃に買ったとんぼ眼鏡、結構流行ったんだけど。
Kore wakai koro ni katta tonbo-megane, kekkō hayatta n' da kedo.
These are a pair of those great big sunglasses that used to be in
  when I was young.

○ とんぼ眼鏡がトレードマークだった女優最近テレビに出なくなっ
たね。
*Tonbo-megane ga torēdomāku datta joyū saikin terebi ni denaku
  natta ne.*
That actress whose trademark was those great big glasses hasn't
  been on TV much lately, has she?

⊱ From the resemblance of the large size and round shape of the glasses
to the eyes of a dragonfly.

蚤　*nomi*　flea

☞　Not on anybody's top-ten list of favorite insects, fleas figure in four
idioms included here, all of which play on its diminutive size rather than
its notorious ability to drive both animals and people crazy, as well as de-
prive them of sleep. Fleas are counted *ippiki* 一匹, when you can find them.

● 蚤の心臓　*nomi no shinzō*　"a flea's heart"
chicken-heartedness, faintheartedness, mousiness, timidity

○ きみの蚤の心臓を鍛えるために肝試しをやろう。
Kimi no nomi no shinzō o kitaeru tame ni kimodameshi o yarō.
Let's see if we can't do something about that yellow belly (candy
  ass) of yours by playing a little game of chicken.

○ 蚤の心臓の持ち主の山田さんが直接社長に抗議したとは大したも
のだ。
*Nomi no shinzō no mochinushi no Yamada-san ga chokusetsu
  shachō ni kōgi shita to wa taishita mono da.*
For someone as lily-livered as Yamada to have complained to the
  boss must have taken a lot of guts.

⊱ From the notion that a flea's heart, presuming they have one, has got
to be miniscule, and the general belief that the size of one's heart is directly related to one's courage. To have the heart of a flea is to be a weenie or a wimp.

● 蚤の夫婦 *nomi no fūfu* "husband and wife fleas"
a little husband and a big wife, Jack Sprat and his wife

○ 中村さんは蚤の夫婦で知られている。
Nakamura-san wa nomi no fūfu de shirarete iru.
The Nakamuras are one of those couples where the wife is bigger than her husband.

○ あの人と結婚したら、蚤の夫婦になっちゃうから二の足踏んじゃうのよね。
Ano hito to kekkon shitara, nomi no fūfu ni natchau kara ni no ashi funjau no yo ne.
I can't see myself getting married to a guy like him who's so much smaller than me.

⚘ From the observation that the female flea is larger than the male. You probably don't want to say it in front of a couple who fit the description. Who knows, the woman might take offense and stomp you.

蜂 *hachi* bee

☞ Bees don't figure in stories that Japanese moms tell their preteen daughters in order to prepare them for life, if they tell them anything. The principal aspects of apian behavior that warrant lexical attention appear to be industriousness, activity, and the ability to inflict pain, though the word for beehive, *hachi no su* 蜂の巣, can be used metaphorically to describe the riddling of something, such as a body lying on the mean streets of Tokyo, with bullet holes. The bee lends its name to a tiny bird as well, the *hachidori* 蜂鳥, or bee bird, which is better known in the West as a hummingbird. The sound bees make when flying is *bunbun* ブンブン or *būn* ブーン. They are counted *ippiki* 一匹.

● 泣き面に蜂 *nakitsura ni hachi* "a bee(sting) on a crying face"
misfortunes seldom come alone; rubbing salt in(to) the wound; adding insult to injury; when it rains, it pours

---

○ 上司に小言を言われ、おまけに帰りに財布を落とすとは泣き面に蜂もいいところだ。
Jōshi ni kogoto o iware, omake ni kaeri ni saifu o otosu to wa nakitsura ni hachi mo ii tokoro da.
Like getting chewed out by my boss wasn't enough, then I had to go and lose my wallet on my way home to boot. Some days you just can't win.

○ 仕事は増えるは、給料は下がるはで、泣きっ面に蜂だもうこりゃ。

Shigoto wa fueru wa, kyūryō wa sagaru wa de, nakittsura ni hachi da mō korya.

More work and less pay. Jeez, this is like adding insult to injury.

○ 今度の円高は日本にとって泣き面に蜂みたいなもんだ。

Kondo no endaka wa Nihon ni totte nakitsura ni hachi mitai na mon da.

The most recent rise in the yen rate is like rubbing salt into the wound for Japan.

🐝 From the notion that someone who is crying is probably already unhappy, and getting stung by a bee on top of that is about as bad as it can get.

● 働き蜂 *hatarakibachi* "a worker bee"

someone who works like a dog, a workhorse, a hard worker, a grind

---

○ 働き蜂と呼ばれる日本人も少しずつ労働時間短縮を目指し始めている。

Hatarakibachi to yobareru Nihon-jin mo sukoshi zutsu rōdō-jikan tanshuku o mezashihajimete iru.

Even the hard-working Japanese are gradually beginning to cut back on the number of hours they work.

○ 連休が終わると家族サービスで疲れきった「働き蜂」たちがオフィスに戻ってきた。

Renkyū ga owaru to kazoku-sābisu de tsukarekitta "hatarakibachi"-tachi ga ofisu ni modotte kita.

The nation's workhorses returned to harness today completely exhausted from a long weekend of "quality time" with their families.

🐝 It's difficult to think of an example for this expression which isn't about the Japanese. The nuance of being a grind is strong, though there is also a sense of industriousness and, perhaps, a slight tinge of resignation as one takes one's place in the traces. Perhaps an important parallel has been overlooked here, for the worker bees that are so often likened to Japanese have all but lost their ability to reproduce, and I've seen figures claiming that if current birthrates in Japan continue, by the year 2050 the population of the nation will dwindle to half its present 125 million or so. Hey guys, take some time to smell the roses.

● 蜂の巣をつついたよう *hachi no su o tsutsuita yō* "like having poked a beehive" be thrown into utter confusion, be a madhouse; commotion

○ 証券業界はそのニュースに蜂の巣をつついたような騒ぎだった。

Shōken-gyōkai wa sono nyūsu ni hachi no su o tsutsuita yō na sawagi datta.

The securities industry was thrown into utter confusion at the news. / All hell broke loose in the securities industry when the news was released.

○ ポケベルの新製品の注文が殺到し、営業部は蜂の巣をつついたようだった。

Pokeberu no shin-seihin no chūmon ga sattō shi, eigyō-bu wa hachi no su o tsutsuita yō datta.

The sales department turned into a madhouse (There was pandemonium in the sales department) when orders for our new pagers started pouring in.

🐝 This is a false friend, for while it may sound like the English idiom "stir up a hornet's nest," there is no sense of creating trouble or arousing anger in the Japanese. Rather, the idiom evokes a sense of the excitement and confusion of jillions of tiny flapping wings when a hive, belonging to a bunch of bees who were minding their own business, has been disturbed.

蛍 *hotaru* firefly

☞ Nature's original "thousand points of light," the two dozen or so species of fireflies found in Japan, especially the luminous ones, have long been thought to embody the souls of the dead. Just how this quaint folk belief squares with decadent romanticists of yesteryear who used the firefly as a metaphor for passionate love remains unclear, for there is no indication that these Heian aristocrats were necrophiles.

One thing that is clear is that most Japanese associate the firefly with the nation's version of "Auld Lang Syne," *Hotaru no Hikari*「蛍の光」. Unfortunately, fireflies are seldom around to be enjoyed in today's urban environment unless you shell out a few bucks to buy a handful at your local friendly department store—which is exactly what some parents are forced to do when summer vacation rolls around and the kids are given their summer homework. The collecting of such insects remains the number one assignment in many grammar schools.

● 蛍族 *hotaru-zoku* "firefly clan"

someone, usually a husband, who has to go out on the veranda to smoke (because of growing concern over the effects of secondary smoke on others, especially children); a glowworm

---

○ この団地も夜になると蛍族があちらこちらに見られる。

Kono danchi mo yoru ni naru to hotaru-zoku ga achira kochira ni mirareru.

The glowworms are out in force around this apartment complex once night falls.

○ 蛍族にとって冬は厳しい。

Hotaru-zoku ni totte fuyu wa kibishii.

Winter's tough on people who have to go out of the house to smoke.

🐚 From the lambent glow of lighted cigarettes in the darkness. A poetic expression in deference to those driven from their homes by spouses and children more interested in longevity than they are.

みみず（蚯蚓） *mimizu* earthworm

☞ Our annelid little buddies have hardly wormed their way into the Japanese lexicon. About all the use they get is as fishbait. But now they're in the news with recent discoveries that, in some areas of Japan, the use of chemical fertilizers, pesticides, and herbicides has been so extensive that the birds eating the beneficial little fellas are starting to drop out of the sky from some kind of poisoning. Some of the more interesting kanji compounds that have been used to write this word include 歌女, or songstress, 地竜, or earth dragon, and 土竜, or dirt dragon. Visions of *Dune*? Earthworms are counted *ippiki* 一匹.

● みみずのぬたくったような字 *mimizu no nutakutta yō na ji* "letters (handwriting) like an earthworm had crawled and squirmed"

one's calligraphy (handwriting) is like hen scratches

○ このみみずのぬたくったような字はあの人に違いない。

Kono mimizu no nutakutta yō na ji wa ano hito ni chigainai.

This scribbling has gotta be hers.

○ 手紙の字はみみずがぬたくったようだったので、彼女は何が書いてあるのか読めなかった。

Tegami no ji wa mimizu ga nutakutta yō datta no de, kanojo wa nani ga kaite aru no ka yomenakatta.

The handwriting in the letter was so squiggly she couldn't make it out.

● みみず腫れ *mimizubare* "an earthworm swelling".
a welt, weal, wheal, wale (or the result of being whaled on);
blister

○ どうしたのその腕のみみず腫れ？
Dō shita no sono ude no mimizubare?
How'd ya get that weal on your arm?

○ 捕虜の背中は一面みみず腫れだった。
Horyo no senaka wa ichimen mimizubare datta.
The prisoner's back was a mass of welts.

🀢 From the resemblance of a wound or blister containing watery matter
to the shape of an earthworm.

虫 *mushi* bug or insect

☞ This is more than a generic term for the whole swarming, buzzing
bunch of little critters that crawl on your screendoor or splatter on your
windshield. It is also the name for internal parasites that inhabit the bodies of animals, and, perhaps by extension and in the absence of any veri-
fiable source of trouble, for the nebulous alien inside us all that has been
attributed with the ability to move us to like or dislike, be angry or mollified. It is also believed to be the source of childhood irritability and other
minor nervous disorders. Insofar as it affects others, attributing responsibility to its peevishness is a way to avoid ascribing responsibility to a
person's actions or decisions. It is used in much in the same way as the
English "seven year itch" to describe a person's inexplicable desire to
cheat on a spouse or lover. In Japanese you awaken the "cheating bug"
uwaki no mushi o okosu 浮気の虫を起こす. The idioms in which *mushi*
appear have been loosely organized into several catagories to expedite
understanding.

虫 *mushi* bug
✦ A. Things the source of which remains uncertain and as-
cribed to some "bug."

● かんの虫 *kan no mushi* "the childhood sickness bug"
a source of peevishness

○ この薬は赤ちゃんのかんの虫によく効きます。
Kono kusuri wa aka-chan no kan no mushi ni yoku kikimasu.
This medicine does wonders for a baby that's always fretting.

○ この子はよく泣くけど、かんの虫でも悪いのだろうか？

Kono ko wa yoku naku kedo, kan no mushi de mo warui no darō ka?

Little thing's always crying. I wonder if maybe she's not just sensitive?

🐝 Actually a kind of childhood nervous disorder, when all else fails you can blame just about any problem an infant might have which leads to crying on this "bug," supposedly inside its tiny body. Hunger, pain, unpleasantness, unease, and diaper rash, all—well almost all—qualify.

● （腹の）虫が納まる　*(hara no) mushi ga osamaru*　"the (stomach) bug settles down"

be satisfied (mollified, placated), cool down, settle down, have one's ruffled feathers smoothed

---

○ 彼が直接謝りに来ない限り虫が納まらない。

Kare ga chokusetsu ayamari ni konai kagiri mushi ga osamaranai.

I'm not going to be satisfied (happy) until he apologizes directly to me.

○ あいつが部長になるのは虫が納まらない。

Aitsu ga buchō ni naru no wa mushi ga osamaranai.

I can't stomach the idea of him (It really gripes me that he's) being promoted to department head.

○ 違法駐車で悩まされていた住人は、警察の一斉取締まりにやっと腹の虫が納まった。

Ihō-chūsha de nayamasarete ita jūnin wa, keisatsu no isseitorishimari ni yatto hara no mushi ga osamatta.

Long troubled by people parking illegally in their neighborhood, residents finally got some relief when the police cracked down. / The police crackdown on illegal parking finally smoothed the local residents' ruffled feathers.

🐝 Whatever the source of the complaint, it's that thing inside that's bugging you that has to be mollified.

● 虫の居所が悪い　*mushi no idokoro ga warui*　"the bug's in a bad place"

be in a bad mood, be in bad humor, be grumpy, be bent (out of shape), be out of sorts; get up on the wrong side of the bed in the morning

---

○ あいつ彼女とでももめて虫の居所が悪いようだ。

Aitsu kanojo to de mo momete mushi no idokoro ga warui yō da.

He must'a got into it with his girlfriend or somethin', the way he's all bent out of shape.

○ 俺のおふくろは虫の居所が悪いとすぐ八つ当たりするんだ。

Ore no ofukuro wa mushi no idokoro ga warui to sugu yatsuatari suru n' da.

My old lady takes it out on everybody when she's feeling out of sorts.

○ ジョンは虫の居所でも悪いんだろう、あんなに怒鳴り散らしてるよ。

Jon wa mushi no idokoro de mo warui n' darō, anna ni donari-chirashite 'ru yo.

I wonder what's bugging John, the way he's dumping on everybody.

✌ The source of the problem is not ascertainable.

● 虫の知らせ *mushi no shirase* 虫が知らせる *mushi ga shiraseru* "the bug lets you know"

(have) a hunch, premonition, funny feeling; just know (something is wrong); feel (something) in *one's* bones

---

○ 虫の知らせで実家に電話したら、祖父が入院したと言うことだった。

Mushi no shirase de jikka ni denwa shitara, sofu ga nyūin shita to iu koto datta.

I called home on a hunch and sure enough my grandfather had been hospitalized. / Something told me to call home, and when I did I discovered that grandpa was sick in the hospital.

○ 虫が知らせたのか、事故を起こした便には乗らずに電車で帰ったので命拾いした。

Mushi ga shiraseta no ka, jiko o okoshita bin ni wa norazu ni densha de kaetta no de inochibiroi shita.

I got this strange feeling and took the train instead of that plane that crashed. I really lucked out.

✌ What native speakers of English feel in their bones, Japanese hear from a bug in their heart. And what they hear is usually bad.

● 虫が好かない *mushi ga sukanai* "the bug doesn't like (it)"

dislike for some reason, just don't like, get bad vibes from, the chemistry's wrong (not there)

○ 虫が好かないんだよなあ、あいつは。
Mushi ga sukanai n' da yo nā, aitsu wa.
There's just something about him that bugs me. / He just rubs me
the wrong way.

○ あの人の言うことはわかるけど、虫が好かないんだよあの言い方が。
*Ano hito no iu koto wa wakaru kedo, mushi ga sukanai n' da yo
ano iikata ga.*
I understand what she's saying, but it's the way she says it that
gets me.

○ あのカフェちょっと気取りすぎて虫が好かないなあ。
Ano kafe chotto kidorisugite mushi ga sukanai nā.
That cafe is a little too hoity-toity for my tastes. I can't get into
going there.

⌘ We've got a near match here with the word bug, as in "Don't bug me,"
which you can still hear occasionally. The Japanese idiom is always encountered in the negative, always of a vague source of dislike, one the
speaker can't seem to pin down.

↪ *uma ga awanai* 馬が合わない

● 泣き虫 *nakimushi* "a crying insect"
a crybaby, a whiner, a big baby; a weenie, pussy, wuss,
wimp

○ 彼がそんな泣き虫だなんて、人は見かけによらないものだ。
*Kare ga sonna nakimushi da nante, hito wa mikake ni yoranai
mono da.*
Who would have ever thought he was such a big baby. Guess you
just can't tell from the way a guy looks.

○ 彼女は飲むと、泣き虫になる。
Kanojo wa nomu to, nakimushi ni naru.
She gets on these crying jags whenever she ties one on.

⌘ Used of a person who cries often or quickly.

● 弱虫 *yowamushi* "a weak insect"
a baby, coward; sissy, pussy, weakling, weenie, wuss,
wimp, candy ass, (of a boy) a momma's boy, a girl

○ 弱虫、毛虫、はさんで捨てろ。

Yowamushi, kemushi, hasande sutero.
Cry baby! Cry baby!

○ そんな弱虫でどうする。
Sonna yowamushi de dō suru.
You're a big sissy aren't ya!

● ～の虫　～ *no mushi* "a bug about (over) *something*"
be into (something), be fanatical (wild/crazy about something), be a fan (of something), live and breathe (something), live (for something / to do something)

○ 彼は本の虫だ。
Kare wa hon no mushi da.
He's a bookworm.

○ 彼女は勉強の虫だ。
Kanojo wa benkyō no mushi da.
She's a grind (powertool). / She's into studying.

○ 子供は遊びの虫だ。
Kodomo wa asobi no mushi da.
Kids love to play. / Kids could play all day. / Kids live to play.

⚘ Used of someone engrossed in one particular activity.

◆ B. Metaphoric use deriving from some characteristically "buggy" trait.

● 虫食い　*mushikui* "insect-eaten"
　1. (literally) insect- (worm-, moth-, etc.) eaten

○ この古文書は虫食い状態で発見された。
Kono komonjo wa mushikui-jōtai de hakken sareta.
This old manuscript was discovered in a worm-eaten condition.

○ このセーターは虫食いがひどいので捨てるしかない。
Kono sētā wa mushikui ga hidoi no de suteru shika nai.
This sweater's so moth-eaten there's nothing to do but throw it out.

---

　2. (metaphorically) partial; broken

○ 用地買収がままならないため、新新幹線ルートは虫食い着工を余儀なくされた。

Yōchi-baishū ga mama naranai tame, shin-shinkansen rūto wa mushikui chakkō o yogi naku sareta.

With procurement of land for new Shinkansen routes not going as well as hoped, the railroad was forced to undertake the construction piecemeal.

○ 工事は今のところ虫食い状態で、いつになったらこの高速が開通するのかまったくわかりませんね。

Kōji wa ima no tokoro mushikui-jōtai de, itsu ni nattara kono kōsoku ga kaitsū suru no ka mattaku wakarimasen ne.

At present, with construction proceeding in fits and starts, there is no telling when the highway will open to traffic.

✌ Used metaphorically of something that proceeds intermittently or is completed in segments that remain disconnected for some time.

● 虫の息　*mushi no iki*　"an insect's breath"

(literally) faint (shallow) breathing; (metaphorically) be (knocking) at death's door, be on *one's* last legs, have had it, be curtains, be all over

---

○ 家族が駆けつけたとき、彼女はすでに虫の息だった。

Kazoku ga kaketsuketa toki, kanojo wa sude ni mushi no iki datta.

She was at death's door when the family made it.

○ 暫定政権はほとんど機能しておらず、もう虫の息だ。

Zantei-seiken wa hotondo kinō shite orazu, mō mushi no iki da.

The provisional government is on its last legs. / It's all over for the provisional government.

○ 彼は虫の息だったが、医者の懸命の努力で奇跡的に命は取り留めた。

Kare wa mushi no iki datta ga, isha no kenmei no doryoku de kiseki-teki ni inochi wa toritometa.

He had one foot in the grave (He was hardly breathing), but the doctor's heroic efforts saved his life.

✌ Used to mean both that one's breathing has all but stopped and that one is close to death for reasons other than those respiratory-related.

✦ C. All right, so everything wouldn't fit in the other categories. Here's the rest.

● 苦虫　*nigamushi*　"a bitter insect"

(~*o (kami)tsubushita yō na kao o suru*) make a sour face;
scowl

○ その議員は不正の証拠を突きつけられ、苦虫を噛みつぶしたよう
な顔を隠せなかった。

Sono giin wa fusei no shōko o tsukitsukerare, nigamushi o kami-tsubushita yō na kao o kakusenakatta.

The Diet member couldn't help grimacing (couldn't hide his displeasure) when presented with the proof of his malfeasance.

○ 言葉につまり、彼は苦虫をつぶした顔をしていた。

Kotoba ni tsumari, kare wa nigamushi o tsubushita kao o shite ita.

Stumped (At a loss for what to say), he got a sour look on his face.

○ 警察官の不祥事に、県警の幹部は釈明の記者会見で終始苦虫をつ
ぶした表情を見せていた。

Keisatsu-kan no fu-shōji ni, kenkei no kanbu wa shakumei no kisha-kaiken de shūshi nigamushi o tsubushita hyōjō o misete ita.

Prefectural police officials, explaining the scandal involving cops under their command, openly showed their distaste for the task throughout the press conference.

○ 彼は過去の失敗を問題にされて苦虫を噛んだ。

Kare wa kako no shippai o mondai ni sarete nigamushi o kanda.

He had to just grin and bear it when someone brought up his past mistakes.

✌ Used of people who are painfully aware their situation is worsening and who find themselves at a loss for words to respond to accusations or the like. The "bitter bug" is chimerical, though almost any insect would probably be sufficiently disgusting to warrant a sour face. The last example features an abbreviated form.

● （悪い）虫がつく　*(warui) mushi ga tsuku*　"a bad bug attaches (itself)"
have (get) a boyfriend (lover)

○ あの娘は、箱入り娘だから虫がつかないように親がいつも目を光
らせている。

Ano ko wa, hakoiri-musume da kara mushi ga tsukanai yō ni oya ga itsumo me o hikarasete iru.

She's led a sheltered life, her parents always making sure there're no guy sniffing around her (that she doesn't get mixed up with some guy).

o 悪い虫でもついたのか、最近彼女帰りが遅いらしいのよ。
Warui mushi de mo tsuita no ka, saikin kanojo kaeri ga osoi rashii no yo.
Maybe she's got a boyfriend. Seems like she's been getting home later and later.

🐝 Used almost exclusively about women, particularly unmarried or widowed ones. Less commonly used of married women who are having an affair. *Warui* appears with the idiom with great regularity.

● 虫のいい   *mushi no ii*   "bug well"
take too much for granted, be asking too much; be all me, me, me

---

o そんな虫のいい話どこにもないよ。
Sonna mushi no ii hanashi doko ni mo nai yo.
You're asking an awful lot there.

o そんな虫のいいことをいって、自分の立場を考えなさい。
Sonna mushi no ii koto o itte, jibun no tachiba o kangaenasai.
You sound like you're taking a lot for granted, but are you really in a position to get all that? / That's all very nice for you, but I mean, who do you think you are?

o 旅行費を出してもらってその上小遣いまでせびるとは虫がよすぎる。
Ryokō-hi o dashite moratte sono ue kozukai made sebiru to wa mushi ga yosugiru.
You're dreamin' if you think we're gonna pay your travel expenses *and* shell out spending money on top of that. / You think we're paying for your trip and giving you pocket money? You've got another think coming.

● 虫も殺さない   *mushi mo korosanai*   "would't kill a bug"
innocent-looking; look as if one could not kill (hurt, harm) a fly (flea)

---

o あの人は取っつきにくいけど、実は虫も殺さないほど優しい人だよ。
Ano hito wa tottsukinikui kedo, jitsu wa mushi o korosanai hodo yasashii hito da yo.
He's a little hard to get to know, but deep down inside he's a big softy (got a heart of gold).

o あいつは虫も殺さない顔して、陰でやることは卑劣なんだから、まあ畳の上では死ねないな。

*Aitsu wa mushi mo korosanai kao shite, kage de yaru koto wa
hiretsu nan da kara, mā tatami no ue de wa shinenai na.*

He's got this innocent look, but the way he's up to no good every
chance he gets, the guy's not gonna die a natural death.

○ あの殺人犯、近所の人の話では、虫も殺さないような人に見えた
らしい。

*Ano satsujin-han, kinjo no hito no hanashi de wa, mushi mo ko-
rosanai yō na hito ni mieta rashii.*

The murderer looked like he wouldn't hurt a fly, according to
what his neighbors were saying.

🦋 Looks are deceptive. That's often the point Japanese want to make
about someone when they begin a sentence with this idiom. Whoever it
is they are talking about is usually not nearly as nice as he makes out to
be. *Mushi mo korosanai kao* 虫も殺さない顔, *mushi mo korosanai yō na
hito* 虫も殺さないような人, and *mushi mo korosanai yō na koto o iu* 虫も
殺さないようなことを言う are all either followed by a comment negating
that image or it is understood by the context that such feelings exist.

● 飛んで火に入る夏の虫   *tonde hi ni iru natsu no mushi* "a
summer insect that has flown into the flames"

(like) a moth drawn to flame, self-destructive; ask for trouble, ask for it

---

○ 彼の行動はまさに「飛んで火に入る夏の虫」であった。

*Kare no kōdō wa masa ni "Tonde hi ni iru natsu no mushi" de
atta.*

He was just asking for trouble the way he was acting.

○ まさか本人が来るとは「飛んで火に入る夏の虫」だな。

*Masaka honnin ga kuru to wa "Tonde hi ni iru natsu no mushi"
da na.*

Who would have ever thought she'd show her face here. She must
have some kind of death wish.

🦋 From the observation that insects drawn to the flame die.

INDEX

動物の慣用句集
ANIMAL IDIOMS

1996年9月20日　第1刷発行

著　者　郷司 正彦
　　　　ジェフ・ガリソン

発行者　野間佐和子

発行所　講談社インターナショナル株式会社
　　　　〒112　東京都文京区音羽 1-17-14
　　　　電話：03-3944-6493

印刷所　株式会社　平河工業社

製本所　株式会社　堅省堂

POWER JAPANESE SERIES

An ongoing series of compact, easy-to-use
guides to essential language skills

ALL ABOUT KATAKANA
カタカナ練習ノート

Anne Matsumoto Stewart

Helps students learn to read and write katakana in a quick,
effective way by combining them into words.

Paperback: 144 pages, ISBN 4-7700-1696-4

ALL ABOUT PARTICLES
助詞で変わるあなたの日本語

Naoko Chino

Discover new particles and remember the old ones, while
learning proper usage. Ideal for study, practice, and
reference.

Paperback: 128 pages, ISBN 4-7700-1501-1

BEYOND POLITE JAPANESE
A Dictionary of Japanese Slang and Colloquialisms
役にたつ話ことば辞典

Akihiko Yonekawa

A concise, pocket-sized reference full of expressions that
all Japanese, but few foreigners, know and use every day.
Sample sentences for every entry.

Paperback: 176 pages, ISBN 4-7700-1539-9

"BODY" LANGUAGE
日本語の中の "ボディ" ランゲージ

Jeffrey G. Garrison

Teaches usage of common idioms that refer to the body
through common colloquial expressions.

Paperback: 128 pages, ISBN 4-7700-1502-X

COMMUNICATING WITH KI
The "Spirit" in Japanese Idioms
「気」の慣用句集
Jeff Garrison and Kayoko Kimiya

Introduces over 200 idioms, all using the word ki, and all essential for communicating in Japanese. Increases the variety of idioms at your command.

Paperback: 144 pages, ISBN 4-7700-1833-9

FLIP, SLITHER, & BANG
Japanese Sound and Action Words
日本語の擬音語・擬態語
Hiroko Fukuda
Translated by Tom Gally

Introduces the most common examples of onomatopoeia through sample sentences and situations—an excellent introduction to colorful language.

Paperback: 128 pages, ISBN 4-7700-1684-0

GONE FISHIN'
New Angles on Perennial Problems
日本語の秘訣
Jay Rubin

Explains, clarifies, and illuminates common trouble spots of the Japanese language in a humorous manner.

Paperback: 128 pages, ISBN 4-7700-1656-5

HOW TO SOUND INTELLIGENT IN JAPANESE
日本語の知的表現
Charles M. De Wolf

Lists, defines, and gives examples of the vocabulary necessary to engage in intelligent conversation in fields such as politics, art, literature, business, and science.

Paperback: 144 pages, ISBN 4-7700-1747-2